Y0-ALC-195

The New York Times

IN THE HEADLINES

Censorship

THE MOTIVES FOR SUPPRESSION

THE NEW YORK TIMES EDITORIAL STAFF

LONGWOOD PUBLIC LIBRARY

Published in 2020 by New York Times Educational Publishing in association with The Rosen Publishing Group, Inc.
29 East 21st Street, New York, NY 10010

Contains material from The New York Times and is reprinted by permission. Copyright © 2020 The New York Times. All rights reserved.

Rosen Publishing materials copyright © 2020 The Rosen Publishing Group, Inc. All rights reserved. Distributed exclusively by Rosen Publishing.

First Edition

The New York Times
Alex Ward: Editorial Director, Book Development
Phyllis Collazo: Photo Rights/Permissions Editor
Heidi Giovine: Administrative Manager

Rosen Publishing
Megan Kellerman: Managing Editor
Alexander Pappas: Editor
Greg Tucker: Creative Director
Brian Garvey: Art Director

Cataloging-in-Publication Data
Names: New York Times Company.
Title: Censorship: the motives for suppression / edited by the New York Times editorial staff.
Description: New York : New York Times Educational Publishing, 2020. | Series: In the headlines | Includes glossary and index.
Identifiers: ISBN 9781642822090 (library bound) | ISBN 9781642822083 (pbk.) | ISBN 9781642822106 (ebook)
Subjects: LCSH: Censorship—Juvenile literature. | Censorship—United States—Juvenile literature. | Freedom of speech—Juvenile literature.
Classification: LCC Z657.C466 2020 | DDC 363.31—dc23

Manufactured in the United States of America

On the cover: One form of censorship is redaction. This is the act of removing text from a document and replacing it with black rectangles to indicate where erasure has taken place; tjhunt/Getty Images.

Contents

8 Introduction

CHAPTER 1

In Times of War: The Suspension of the Free Press

11 The War-Censorship Nuisance. BY THE NEW YORK TIMES

13 Plans for America: A War Censorship SPECIAL TO THE NEW YORK TIMES

16 An Effective Censorship. BY THE NEW YORK TIMES

18 Censorship and Publicity. BY THE NEW YORK TIMES

19 Censorship Bill Fought in House SPECIAL TO THE NEW YORK TIMES

22 War Censorship BY THE NEW YORK TIMES

24 The Censor Defends the Censorship BY BYRON PRICE

31 Censorship Bureau Comes to an End SPECIAL TO THE NEW YORK TIMES

32 War Censorship Discussed by U.S. SPECIAL TO THE NEW YORK TIMES

34 Conflicting Censorship Upsets Many Journalists
BY MALCOLM W. BROWNE

CHAPTER 2

The Role of Censorship in Authoritarian Regimes

37 Stealth Censorship in Venezuela BY DANIEL LANSBERG-RODRÍGUEZ

41 The New Dictators Rule by Velvet Fist BY SERGEI GURIEV AND DANIEL TREISMAN

45 Egypt Officials Stop Facebook Program for Free Access to Internet BY KAREEM FAHIM

47 How Egypt Crowdsources Censorship BY YASMINE EL RASHIDI

52 Turks Click Away, but Wikipedia Is Gone BY PATRICK KINGSLEY

55 Erdogan's Next Target as He Restricts Turkey's Democracy: The Internet BY CARLOTTA GALL

61 Reuters Publishes Account of Myanmar Massacre After Journalists' Arrests BY RICHARD C. PADDOCK

64 Why Are So Many Democracies Breaking Down? BY MICHAEL ALBERTUS AND VICTOR MENALDO

69 The Website That Shows How a Free Press Can Die BY PATRICK KINGSLEY AND BENJAMIN NOVAK

CHAPTER 3

In the Arts, Sciences and More

76 Is There Censorship? BY RACHEL DONADIO

83 Crying Censorship BY STANLEY FISH

87 Bullying and Censorship BY THE NEW YORK TIMES

88 'Censors At Work,' By Robert Darnton BY ALBERTO MANGUEL

93 Australian Furor Over Chinese Influence Follows Book's Delay
BY JACQUELINE WILLIAMS

97 Art Censorship at Guantánamo Bay BY ERIN THOMPSON

99 Seeing Terror Risk, U.S. Asks Journals to Cut Flu Study Facts
BY DENISE GRADY AND WILLIAM J. BROAD

104 Science and Censorship: A Duel Lasting Centuries
BY WILLIAM J. BROAD

109 Don't Censor Influenza Research BY HOWARD MARKEL

112 Anti-Vaccine Activists Have Taken Vaccine Science Hostage
BY MELINDA WENNER MOYER

117 Conservatives Fail the N.F.L.'s Free Speech Test BY DAVID FRENCH

120 Australian Gag Order Stokes Global Debate on Secrecy
BY DAMIEN CAVE

CHAPTER 4
Social and Political Issues in the Internet Age

125 A World Map to Outwit Web Censors BY JOAN OLECK

128 Clearing Out the App Stores: Government Censorship Made Easier BY FARHAD MANJOO

133 In Trump Era, Censorship May Start in the Newsroom
BY JIM RUTENBERG

138 How Important Is Freedom of the Press? BY NATALIE PROULX

141 Google Employees Protest Secret Work on Censored Search Engine for China BY KATE CONGER AND DAISUKE WAKABAYASHI

145 The Dangers of Digital Activism BY MANAL AL-SHARIF

148 There May Soon Be Three Internets. America's Won't Necessarily Be the Best. BY THE NEW YORK TIMES

153 The Poison on Facebook and Twitter Is Still Spreading
BY THE NEW YORK TIMES

157 The Problem With Banning Pornography on Tumblr
BY JESSICA POWELL

CHAPTER 5

Case Studies in Russia, China and Saudi Arabia

160 Who Likes Web Censorship? (Ask Putin.) BY MARJORIE CONNELLY

162 'They Want to Block Our Future': Thousands Protest Russia's Internet Censorship BY NEIL MACFARQUHAR

166 Russia, Accused of Faking News, Unfurls Its Own 'Fake News' Bill BY LINCOLN PIGMAN

169 In Russia, a Top University Lacks Just One Thing: Students
BY IVAN NECHEPURENKO

175 Ai Weiwei: How Censorship Works BY AI WEIWEI

180 After Criticism, Publisher Reverses Decision to Bow to China's Censors BY CHRIS BUCKLEY

183 China's Oppression Reaches Beyond Its Borders BY LAUREN HILGERS

187 Twitter Users in China Face Detention and Threats in New Beijing Crackdown BY PAUL MOZUR

192 Netflix's Bow to Saudi Censors Comes at a Cost to Free Speech
BY JIM RUTENBERG

197 A Warning to Saudis About What Happens to Dissidents
THE NEW YORK TIMES

199 C.I.A. Concludes That Saudi Crown Prince Ordered Khashoggi Killed BY JULIAN E. BARNES

203 Saudi King Stands by Crown Prince as Outrage Over Khashoggi Killing Spreads BY BEN HUBBARD AND CARLOTTA GALL

208 The War on Truth Spreads BY THE NEW YORK TIMES

211 Glossary
213 Media Literacy Terms
215 Media Literacy Questions
217 Citations
222 Index

Introduction

DISTILLED TO ITS most basic purpose, censorship is an instrument of suppression. Loosely defined as "the suppression or prohibition of any parts of books, films, news, etc. that are considered obscene, politically unacceptable or a threat to security," the term has come to encompass far more in our collective history. For as long as information and ideas have been disseminated, authoritative powers have actively sought to censure those who spread notions and facts that would impede their purposes. Such powers would justify this suppression by arguing that some ideas and truths not only upset the status quo but are an attack on the state itself. In this sense, censorship has become a convenient weapon to silence any presumed opposition.

The ever-fraught relationship between the censor and the censored in the United States is uniquely emblematic in this struggle. Enshrined in the First Amendment of the Constitution is the oft-referenced clause: "Congress shall make no law respecting an establishment of religion, or prohibiting the free exercise thereof; or abridging the freedom of speech, or of the press." The United States was the first Western government to officially afford any such protection of the written or spoken word; however, the nation's short history has already demonstrated the intricate and contradictory enforcement of this founding pillar of the American free press.

Nowhere else is this better demonstrated than in times of war. Wherein times of peace the government has maintained a degree of zealous protection for the rights of its citizens to speak their minds, history has demonstrated that during social and martial conflict this stance is quickly reversed. Indeed, wartime censorship has often

SEYMOUR CHWAST

been actively encouraged by members of the press itself — sometimes with unfortunate consequences. This imposed self-censorship is prevalent in the modern age as well.

In today's world, censorship is better known for a more nefarious purpose. Authoritarian regimes have long used censorship not only as a tool to quell threats to the state, but to silence all forms of criticism. So often, this form of censorship can become a practice of censoring authors entirely: Journalists and other writers, critical of regime policies and practices, not only run the risk of incurring censorship from states — they hazard their lives. The recent case of Jamal Khashoggi's state-sanctioned murder by elements of the Saudi Arabian government is such an example.

With the advent of the Internet and global access to information, digital censorship has increased. Ever wary of technological advancement and the greater accessibility of once privileged information, governments throughout the world have enacted various incarnations of digital censorship to better manage the flow of data. Corporations have also played a role in this dynamic, such as Google's and Apple's business dealings with the Chinese government. While these relationships can be profitable for both parties, they can also compromise ethical obligations and moral standards.

While censorship is often seen as an antiquated historical construct, it is indeed alive today. Whether it is the suppression of a government study on influenza or the shuttering of a burlesque satire on a former dictator, censorship remains prevalent in today's world.

CHAPTER 1

In Times of War: The Suspension of the Free Press

While people may decry the moral ambiguity around any curtailment of thought or collective belief in times of peace, armed conflict has often fostered a far different reaction. War and times of upheaval are often catalysts for the rise of censorship. Concealing or omitting information can protect military efforts abroad; however, it can also jeopardize foreign relations and the public's trust in their government.

The War-Censorship Nuisance.

BY THE NEW YORK TIMES | APRIL 10, 1862

THE FOLLOWING IS transmitted to the Philadelphia *Inquirer* "by authority of Gen. Wool:"

> A circular, issued by the rebels, was found by one of Gen. Hamilton's Aids. The purport of it was a full description of the present onward movement, with all the details; also, Gen. Magruder's plan of defeating the Union programme. The enemy must have received this information from a high source several weeks ago, or they could not have got the circular out so soon.

We submit to the Secretary of War the propriety of at once suspending all restrictions upon the publication of war news. We have his own statement that the censorship was established to protect the forward movement of Gen. McClellan. The Press, at an incalculable cost, has complied with the rules of the Department, and yet the only result is, that loyal people have been kept in the dark about matters touching which the rebeldom has been flooded with light. The last excuse for the embargo has vanished. If, after the bit of evidence we reproduce, it be still maintained, it will be a gratuitous abuse of official authority, deserving the utmost popular indignation.

Plans for America: A War Censorship

SPECIAL TO THE NEW YORK TIMES | **JAN. 3, 1916**

Gen. Scott, Chief of Staff, recommends commission, to act whenever necessary.

WASHINGTON, JAN. 2. — The annual report of Major Gen. Hugh L. Scott, Chief of Staff of the army, draws many deductions from the war that deal with changes needed in the equipment and organization of the army. One of the most important of his recommendations looks to the establishment of a commission to draft regulations for a general censorship to be adopted in time of war. This commission would consist of an army officer and a naval officer, who would be required to consult with representatives of press associations and managers of the leading newspapers in the country. On this subject the report says:

> At present there is no well devised plan for regulating or controlling the censorship of messages that may come into the hands of army and navy officers in time of war. The General Staff of the army has submitted in this regard the following recommendations:
>
> '(A) — That an officer of the army designated by the Secretary of War and an officer designated by the Secretary of the Navy to be directed to consult with representatives of the press associations and managers of leading newspapers of the country in drafting legislation authorizing the President to issue regulations for control of publication and censorship of telegraph, cable, wireless mail communications wherever such course may seem to him necessary for the defense of the country.
>
> '(B) — That such draft, after approval by the Judge Advocate General of the army, either be submitted to Congress at once or held ready to submit when conditions seem to warrant favorable action, as the President may deem proper.

CAREFUL PLANS URGED.

> '(C) — That, whether or not such draft be now submitted, regulations to render an effective censorship be drawn up and careful plans be

prepared for execution of censorship under such regulations. These should include a record of each cable, telegraph and wireless station which would require supervision by a censor; list of all newspapers, periodicals and correspondents; selection of army and navy officers, preferably retired, and of experienced newspaper men as personnel of the censorate. Following the British plan, the Assistant Secretary of War could well be assigned as director of the censorate.

'(D) — In time of national peril and absence of legislation, the President should at once direct a censorship of all communication by mail, cable, wire or wireless; if necessary, declaring martial law to an extent necessary to effect arbitrary suppression of publication or communication of matter that might prove detrimental to national defense or useful to a possible enemy.'

It is of vital importance that all these steps be taken before the occasion arises for application of a censorship. We may anticipate greater confusion and dissatisfaction than Great Britain experienced if no plans be prepared and no personnel be selected for execution thereof until the time arrives when censorship and control of the press become as necessary as in Europe in 1914.

The report devotes a great deal of attention to artillery, which has played so important a part in the great war. The Chief of Staff recommends the use of guns not smaller than 12 inches in calibre, drawn on railway carriages or dragged by motor trucks, for use along the coast in repelling attack. While the report does go into details, it seems to look to the installation of a system of defense like that proposed by Lawrence Luellan of 220 West Nineteenth Street, New York, as described with an accompanying illustration in The New York Times of this morning.

MORE MACHINE GUNS.

Newspaper dispatches from Europe have stressed the use by the Germans of machine guns. While General Scott does not discuss any of the foreign armies by name, he does say that it is as a result of observations abroad that the General Staff has decided to increase the number of machine guns attached to each infantry regiment to seven. This change will be effected as fast as the guns are made.

The General Staff seems to think that officers will be found for a reserve army, should such an organization be established. In the year certificates were issued to thirty-seven persons found by examination to be "specially qualified to hold commissions in any volunteer force which may hereafter be called for." In addition, about 1,400 students at schools receiving military instruction under army officers have been recommended, subject to physical examination, as qualified. Besides all these, more than 5,000 men have applied for volunteer commissions, or a total of about 7,000.

On the other hand, the army reserve declined in strength by one man in the year, so that on June 30, 1914, it numbered only sixteen, just the number invited to dinner here one night several months ago by Representative Gardner of Massachusetts. Under the operation of the new law increases in this force did not begin before Nov. 1, and results since that date are not accounted for in the report.

An Effective Censorship.

BY THE NEW YORK TIMES | MARCH 10, 1917

IT IS NECESSARY, of course, that measures be taken to prevent the transmission abroad of information that would imperil the success of the efforts of our Government to defend out commercial rights upon the sea. The Navy Department has appealed to American newspapers not to publish any information concerning the armament or the dates of departure of ships, and it has appealed to cable companies to suppress all information about the sailings of ships crossing the Atlantic in either direction.

To prevent the publishing here of information of this nature would be a resource of very doubtful value. Thousands of persons who are in this country will know of the sailings of ships, they will have information about the arming of merchant ships. Any spy or other person having a motive for transmitting such information abroad could easily accomplish his purpose by sending some apparently harmless message which might convey information quite other than that to be derived from its words used in their ordinary meaning. The purpose of the Government can be best accomplished, can be accomplished only, by preventing the transmission abroad of information quite harmless here, information which in fact will be pretty generally disseminated here. Censorship can be made effective only in the cable offices and wireless stations and in the office of land telegraph lines on the Mexican border. It will be necessary to scrutinize with the utmost care all messages and communications open to suspicion or coming from sources not known to be responsible. The means of sending information out of the country should have the attention of the censor rather than the ordinary channels of domestic publicity.

The matter is going to be one of very great importance. As we know, the function of the censor exercised ignorantly, arbitrarily, or capriciously may do a great deal of needless harm. To escape the errors of the censorship abroad, it would be wise for the War and Navy Departments, before devising their regulations, to take counsel with those who from abundant experience are competent to indicate not only the methods of censorship that are quite superfluous, but also the loopholes which may render a seemingly rigid censorship quite ineffective.

Censorship and Publicity.

BY THE NEW YORK TIMES | APRIL 16, 1917

WHILE THERE IS as yet no press censorship law, and the Espionage bill, so drawn as surreptitiously to create a press censorship, has not yet reached a vote, while, indeed, the only existing authority on the subject is the mandate of the Constitution directing the Congress to pass no law abridging the freedom of the press, three members of the Cabinet have addressed to the President a communication recommending the creation of a Committee on Public Information, combining the two functions of "censorship and publicity"; and the President has appointed the committee, including the three Cabinet officers and a civilian Chairman, Mr. George Creel.

Mr. Creel may have been unjustly criticised in Denver, but we are unable to discover in his turbulent career as a municipal officer there, or in his qualities as a writer, or in his services to the Woman Suffrage Party in New York, any evidence of the ability, the experience, or the judicial temperament required "to gain the understanding and co-operation of the press," as the three Cabinet officers put it. That he is qualified for any position of authority over the press is made further doubtful by his publicly expressed hostility toward certain newspapers.

As to "rallying the authors of the country," the other function assigned to Mr. Creel, those estimable and gifted ladies and gentlemen can doubtless be made useful in various ways, but essential to the information of the public during the war will be not pleasing fictions prepared by imaginative writers but facts, even painful facts, accurately described by conscientious and competent reporters.

Censorship Bill Fought in House

SPECIAL TO THE NEW YORK TIMES | MAY 1, 1917

WASHINGTON, APRIL 30. — The House began consideration today of the Espionage bill. There was immediate objection to the censorship section, which is construed by many members as interfering with the right of free speech and a free press. Although the house bill is more liberal in this respect than the Senate measure, Chairman Webb of the Judiciary Committee was subjected to many questions by members who feared the section might be misinterpreted because of its seeming ambiguity. Representative Mann, the minority leader; Representatives Madden and McCormick of Illinois, and Walsh of Massachusetts were among the members insisting that the proposed law should clearly define the right of criticism during the period of the war.

Section 4 of the House bill provides that during war or threatened war the President by proclamation may prohibit "the publishing or communicating of or the attempting to publish or communicate any information relating to the national defense which, in his judgment, is of such character that it is or might be useful to the enemy; provided, that nothing in this section shall be construed to limit or restrict any comment, discussion or criticism of the acts or policies of the Government or its representatives, or the publication of the same."

"The bill says the President 'in his judgment' may prohibit this," said Mr. McCormick, "but this means that some Minister of the President will make the decision. The President hasn't time for all those details."

LOOKS FAR INTO THE FUTURE.

"The newspapers are good now," replied Mr. Volstead of Minnesota, ranking Republican of the Judiciary Committee, "but some newspapers may begin the publication of improper matter if the war continues for a year or more. We should protect the good newspapers by making others respect these things. Suppose the war drags along, there is bound to be some dissatisfaction, and improper comment must be held down."

Mr. Walsh, another Republican member of the committee, expressed the opinion that the newspapers were patriotic enough to maintain a voluntary censorship, as they are now doing.

"The newspapers do not want to be disturbed in their liberty of speech," said Chairman Webb, "but I hope we will remember that this is a time of war, and while men are giving their lives and money the newspapers should at least be willing to give up their right, if it is a right, to publish those things which the President may regard as hurtful to the country and useful to the enemy."

"Did you write this bill on the theory that the Constitution is operative during the war?" asked Mr. Fess of Ohio. Mr. Webb replied affirmatively, and said he did not think the censorship section was unfair to the press or that it would be unreasonably administered.

"The bill says 'in his judgment,' " said the minority leader, Mr. Mann. "This language does not seem to be explicit. Is it the purpose that the President shall specify the information that is not to be published? That cannot be done, of course."

"The President can do it much better than we can by legislation," said Mr. Webb.

"The President would not specify information that could not be published, because that itself would be publication of it," said Mr. Mann.

POSSIBLE TO BE EXPLICIT.

"He can specify the character of the information — such as the movement of troops and vessels, and things of that sort," replied Mr. Webb. Mr. Mann insisted that anything that could be embraced in a proclamation could be put into the law. If the Departments of War and Justice were able to frame a proclamation for the President, he asked, why could they not frame a law that specified what may and may not be published, so there would be no uncertainty? Mr. Webb argued that a new situation might arise which a statutory provision would not meet.

Mr. Madden said: "The American people are going to furnish men and money to fight this war, and they ought to have information concerning the conduct of the war. This bill is one of the most important ever to come before the American Congress, because it affects the liberties of the people as never before."

Under a rigid interpretation of the law, Mr. Madden said, it might prove impossible for a newspaper or any other agency to disseminate information concerning unsatisfactory conditions in the army, such as the lack of proper food, clothing and equipment.

Mr. Huddleston of Alabama asked if "representatives" of the Government meant army officers, and if criticisms of such officers would be permissible. Mr. Webb said he thought they were "representatives," but Mr. Huddleston doubted this, saying they were rather the agents of the Government.

The bill will be debated further tomorrow.

War Censorship

EDITORIAL | BY THE NEW YORK TIMES | NOV. 24, 1942

A DELICATE PROBLEM of war censorship is raised by the mutual complaints of British correspondents in America and American correspondents in Britain. British correspondents here say that the American censorship will not let them send to their countries full accounts of criticisms here of British war policy. American correspondents make a like complaint about their inability fully to report British criticisms of America.

It is not difficult to understand the motives of the censors. Recriminations across the ocean would endanger that harmony between the American and British war effort so essential to victory. But censorship of mutual criticism could easily have the opposite of the effect intended. It is good to know what our Allies think of our war policies. If these are wrong or mistaken we may change them in time. We may prevent a minor difference from growing unchecked into a serious one. Both the American and the British censors should reconsider their policy from this point of view. Censorship of a sort is certainly needed. But it should be mainly a voluntary censorship practiced by the critics themselves and by the correspondents who cable the criticisms. The kind of criticism in which either Americans or Englishmen say to each other: "We are better than you; we are doing more in the war effort than you are; we are more efficient; our policies are morally noble and yours are morally dubious" can result only in dissension and harm. Mutual candor, if it is to be helpful, must rest on mutual tact and on basic mutual esteem.

Factual censorship presents less difficult problems than censorship of mutual criticism. The only good reason for suppressing facts in wartime is that their publication would help the enemy. There has been a highly gratifying trend recently toward more frankness on the part of the Navy. This frankness has improved American morale.

In some directions it could profitably go farther. Certainly this is the time, if ever, to publish an accumulation of bad news hitherto withheld from the American people. This is the time to publish a fuller account of the naval damage at Pearl Harbor; to tell us how many planes were destroyed at Pearl Harbor and in the Philippines. Even if the Japanese do not have a shrewd idea of how much airplane damage they did on those occasions nearly a year ago, the information could be of no possible use to them today.

With the war news in every theatre running so heavily in favor of the United Nations as it has been in recent weeks, there is no danger in this country today of despair. There is no danger of defeatism. The only danger is overconfidence. Members of the Administration still lash out against the "rumor mongers." But rumors circulate and are credited among a people only when that people feel that they are not getting the truth. Give them the truth, let them feel that they are getting the truth, and rumors will dissolve like a fog under a strong sun.

The Censor Defends the Censorship

BY BYRON PRICE | FEB. 11, 1945

Byron Price, the Director of Censorship, replies to those who complain that too much news is kept from the public.

HOW ACCURATE AND complete is our war news? How well is John Doe, here at home, informed about the lot and fortunes of GI Joe at the front? Is too much of the truth stopped in the name of security?

These questions recently have stirred widespread discussion. They are important questions, and there is no short and simple answer to them. The difficulty of projecting a precise impression of events through space, even between two persons in the same room, is well understood. Mankind, we are told, is destined at best to see through a glass darkly, and war sets many strange designs on the windowpane. No one will ever know what a war is like unless he is there and sees for himself; and even then he will know only a part of the story. But that is no reason why the best possible effort should not be made to give the home front as much news as security will permit.

As this discussion mounts, it is only natural that the censor should become a target for castigation. All of the old reliables — "senseless," "idiotic," "asinine," "bureaucratic," and the rest — have been resurrected and launched broadside at Censorship and all its works.

Much of this is understandable and some of it deserved. Censorship never can be an exact science. It is an integral part of war, and no war can be fought without accidents and errors and confusions. One of the anomalies, however, is that no one has charged Censorship with being too liberal and thus helping the enemy to prolong the war. The shoe is on the other foot. At a time of belt-tightening for manpower, production and rationing, when new and more severe restrictions are elbowing travelers off the trains and pushing down the thermostat in American homes, an opposite trend is proposed in many quarters for Censorship.

The longer the war lasts, the more vocal is the demand for less censorship, not more.

It takes no great amount of reflection to expose the fallacy of such thinking. Censorship's responsibility is to help protect the life of the nation, and if the war has turned out to be longer and tougher than we expected, then surely there is need for increased vigilance. Thus far the correspondents on the firing line and the newspapers and broadcasters at home have done a fabulously successful job of protecting the national security. They scarcely can afford, in the national interest or in their own interest, to relax or become careless now. It is not a time to take a chance.

IT IS A TIME for even-tempered reflection, not hysteria. It is denied by no one that Censorship, which is contrary to all American principles, is a necessary nuisance in wartime. Protests against it are natural on the part of a free press, and no one should resent them. But neither Censorship issues nor any of the other grave issues of these troubled days can be solved wisely on a basis of hasty conclusions and intemperate epithet. The problems are far too important for that.

The plain and sober truth of the matter is that in no war in history and in no country in the world has the common man been given access to such detailed and comprehensive reports of warfare as those which are placed hourly before the readers of American newspapers and the listeners beside American radios. If, upon reflection, that statement needs proof, it can be found in ample measure by laying today's newspaper alongside the newspaper of 1918, or 1864, or any other wartime you may select. For the first time in history not a few, but literally hundreds, of American correspondents have opportunity to roam the battlefields under the fire of the enemy, and even to sit in council with the higher military authorities and learn in the briefing-room of battle plans which still are in the making. In what previous war, as in this one, have thirty correspondents given up their lives to the cause of public information?

But this is not, of course, the whole of the matter. The plain fact is, also, that these reporters are not permitted by Censorship to write all they know or describe all they see. Naturally. However you may qualify it, no rational person can escape the truth of a fundamental tenet of all censorship, namely, that once a piece of news has been published widely, it must be assumed that the enemy has been informed. Actually, in these days of widespread use of interceptible radio for press transmission the enemy doubtless reads most American dispatches from the front long before those same dispatches become available to newspaper subscribers at home. In these circumstances no responsible commanding general, with the lives of his men and the fortunes of his country resting on his judgment, can fail to be anxious eternally that the enemy be not told too much.

WHAT IT COMES down to, then, is a problem of degree. How much should be withheld? As this is written most of the criticism of Censorship hinges on an assumption that too much unpleasant news is kept from the American public. The issue has many angles which cannot all be embraced in moderate space. A conspicuous example, which will serve as well as another, is the storm of discussion centering about the December German breakthrough in Belgium and Luxembourg. It was charged that in that instance censors operating under General Eisenhower suppressed too much. Naturally, all of the facts about that are not yet available, but many of them are.

The charges came from various sources. No attempt will be made here to consider the pronouncements of traveling salesmen and visiting firemen who, after a day or two or a week or two in contact with the rear areas of the war in Europe, came home and began lecturing as experts in military security and censorship. Nor is it necessary to engage in debate with the editorial writers of home-town newspapers who automatically, at the first alarm, wheeled out the old artillery of abusive adjectives without taking the pains or having the means to look into the matter and ascertain the facts.

THERE IS ONE GROUP of witnesses, however, whose experience and whose magnificent record of sacrifices and service more than entitles them to a respectful hearing. They are the group of American correspondents who formally protested at General Eisenhower's headquarters in France that too much about the German military thrust was suppressed.

The core of that complaint was that the correspondents were prohibited from reporting exactly what towns were in German hands. This was information, it was argued, already possessed by the German High Command, and it was information which the American public should have in order to understand the extent and stark potentialities of the attack.

The reasoning was sound, certainly, provided the premise was correct. But on this latter point some difficulty arises. Obviously we do not know and probably never will know how much detailed information was available at German headquarters. And it must be a matter of opinion also to what degree the public in this country realized the danger and how much that realization would have been aided by the addition of certain specific place names. Certain it is that streamer headlines in the newspapers and graphic announcements over the radio reminded the nation hour by hour of the sweeping reversal of events at the fighting front. No charge was made, in fact, that the military commanders were seeking to conceal the general seriousness of the situation.

CONSIDERING THAT SITUATION as a whole, no one will say that the problems wrapped up in it were easy of solution. The struggle was not a single battle. It was many battles spread over an almost chaotic scene of fanning columns, divided by hills, woods and streams. Units were isolated on both sides. Parachutists were dropped behind the lines; and it is worthy of note that one captured German paratroop officer complained in hot anger that the Nazi radio had reported the town where he descended already in German hands. The information was incorrect,

Byron Price.

and the paratroop command was virtually wiped out. In this instance, at least, a true and detailed statement of the facts would have meant fewer dead Germans.

The conflicting estimates of the situation retailed day by day in the German broadcasts and even in the German official communiqués furnish additional testimony that the enemy was guessing. Very often the purpose of these guesses has been to exert deliberate pressure on Allied commanders to disclose the true state of affairs. An interesting observation (proving that not all editorial writers follow a blind assumption that all censorship is wrong), appeared recently in The Corpus Christi (Texas) Caller. Remarking that the Germans at first estimated American prisoners taken in the Belgium-Luxembourg salient at 40,000 and then reduced the figure to 24,000, The Caller said; "They deliberately fish for information, mistrusting their own figures, and as long as our command refuses to take the cork under, they cannot be sure."

We had great military movements of our own to conceal from the enemy. Three days after the start of the German attack General Patton was ordered to take immediate command of a bold counter-action on the southern flank of the German indentation. This meant thinning his own lines on other fronts. It meant gathering and grouping a great mass of men and material. To the north another large attack was organizing under Marshal Montgomery. A strong argument can be made that secrecy was absolutely vital, even as to the results of the first days of the actual counter-attack, so that the enemy could not grasp the full meaning and weight of our concentrations.

NOR CAN WE omit from a judicial review of events one other circumstance always characteristic of war. The sudden German stroke presented a new, disorganizing threat of the most frightful potentialities. At such times, military machinery does not operate like clockwork. The censors on the spot were, of course, Army officers responsible to General Eisenhower. Commanders down to the lowest officer had to make decisions quickly, desperately. In matters of security they could not have known just where they were. Their wholly natural disposition was to take no chance whatever. The equally natural disappointment of the correspondents may well have magnified itself in this atmosphere of extreme tension and uncertainty, and no one could be blamed for that.

Interesting in this situation is the fact that dispatches severely critical of Allied intelligence and preparedness, and the most unrestrained accounts of battlefield horror, continued to come out of the imperiled sector without interference from the military censors. And all of this was published and broadcast in every American community.

THE CENTRAL ISSUE must, in the end, come down to a matter of opinion since many of the variables cannot be resolved. So far as the public was concerned only one attempt to survey reaction actually was made, and the results may be set down here for whatever they are worth. The Office of Public Opinion Research, a private fact-finding agency, reported that it had conducted such a canvass of popular sentiment, stating the exact complaint of the correspondents and asking whether they should have been permitted to write in greater detail. Of those questioned, 7 per cent strangely enough had no opinion, 24 per cent agreed with the correspondents and 69 per cent said the information should have been withheld if the Army felt disclosure would handicap military operations.

Such is the tangled background of what may go down in history as a celebrated controversy over censorship. What is the lesson? It would take a better man than Solomon to render an unassailable verdict, but one thing surely is clear enough: Censorship is a complex business, dealing in the most dangerous of wares, and its problems are not to be solved wisely by bombast and curbstone opinion.

Censorship Bureau Comes to an End

SPECIAL TO THE NEW YORK TIMES | NOV. 16, 1945

WASHINGTON, NOV. 15 — After a life of one month and four days less than four years, the war-created Bureau of Censorship went out of existence tonight. Byron Price, the director, and the remaining seventy of the staff, turned over the keys of their desks, already tagged for delivery to other Federal agencies.

At its peak the bureau employed 14,500 persons, with 800 to 900 in Washington. Besides supervising a voluntary censorship by newspapers and radio, it inspected millions of tons of mail.

Begun Dec. 19, 1941, twelve days after Pearl Harbor, actual censorship ceased Aug. 15, three days after V-J Day. Since then the bureau has been liquidating itself.

Mr. Price, former executive news editor of The Associated Press, has made no plans beyond taking a rest.

War Censorship Discussed by U.S.

SPECIAL TO THE NEW YORK TIMES | AUG. 16, 1965

WASHINGTON, AUG. 15 — Gen. Earle G. Wheeler, Chairman of the Joint Chiefs of Staff, said today that the United States would study the possibility of imposing military censorship in Vietnam.

In a television interview, General Wheeler touched on a United States military complaint from Saigon about a news dispatch telling of the movement of United States units to relieve the besieged camp at Ducco.

General Wheeler said that such information was valuable to the enemy and could cause "a bloody defeat for our forces, or it might permit the Vietcong to escape a trap."

Asked whether he favored military censorship to replace the present voluntary system whereby United States newsmen in Vietnam withhold certain types of information, General Wheeler said:

"I think we are going to have to take a very hard look at this."

Indicating the he believed the present system was unsatisfactory, he added: "I feel that we must find the means to make sure that this kind of thing doesn't happen again."

SAYS CHINA MOVES TROOPS

In the television interview on "Issues and Answers," broadcast by the American Broadcasting Company, General Wheeler said Communist China had moved air units, though not in large numbers, nearer to the borders with Vietnam.

The Chinese have also strengthened their air forces on Hainan Island, he said, but no sizable movement of ground troops has taken place.

Discussing press coverage of Vietnam fighting, General Wheeler said United States officials had worked hard to improve "what has been, in my judgment, a most unsatisfactory situation."

The general, who conceded that he was not an expert on the subject, said the situation might be a result "of having some young men, relatively inexperienced men, in the field."

On the other hand, he said, "invariably when known people — that is, men and women who have made their mark in the new profession — go out there ... the reporting is of a very high caliber."

The Ducco dispatch about which General Wheeler complained was sent out and then killed last week by United Press International. It described the sending of two units from Saigon to the Ducco area which was then the center of intensive fighting. A similar dispatch was sent by the Columbia Broadcasting System.

A Defense Department source said today that these dispatches sent before the troop movement was completed, could have done serious damage. In fact, he said, no damage had been done so far as could be determined.

United States newsmen in Saigon have agreed to withhold information regarding troop movements until it is authorized. They also withhold specific descriptions of the size or type of units fighting. They are not furnished with casualty figures on specific engagements.

Conflicting Censorship Upsets Many Journalists

BY MALCOLM W. BROWNE | JAN. 21, 1991

DHAHRAN, SAUDI ARABIA, JAN. 20 — Many news correspondents covering the war with Iraq are bridling under a system of conflicting rules and confusing censorship.

For the first time since World War II, correspondents must submit to near-total military supervision of their work.

The men and women covering the war are permitted to see and hear a great deal as members of pools who are given access to military sites. But they may not use place names or other clues that could help the Iraqis. Most accept such constraints without protest, but there have been instances when information that correspondents were ordered to withhold was made available soon after by officers in Washington.

This reporter encountered a telling example of the paradoxical censorship rules in a pool assignment last week, when officers on the scene said American forces had destroyed laboratories where the Iraqis were thought to be developing a nuclear potential.

BEST NEWS FROM THE TOP

Permission to report the attacks — a major development — was denied by the unit commander, who said the information could assist Iraqi intelligence operations and should be withheld. Correspondents complied, but the information was later reported in detail by the American military commanders during their daily briefing in Saudi Arabia. The Pentagon is clearly eager to be the first to report the most newsworthy information.

Seemingly haphazard application of censorship rules has blanked out or truncated the timely release of some important articles even after they survived the required military "security review." In other cases, information deemed dangerous to American troops by commanders in the field has been cleared by the Pentagon and published or broadcast.

Most journalists here agree that military information officers at the Joint Information Bureau in Dhahran are helpful and fair. Many of the problems correspondents face originate in Washington, they say.

About 60 pool reporters selected from several hundred men and women covering the Persian Gulf campaign must share their dispatches and video and radio tapes with all their colleagues. The pool reporters go out in small groups, usually six reporters and camera operators, to some American unit on land or shipboard to observe activity. But the service men and women selected for interviews by pool members are chosen by information officers accompanying each pool, in cooperation with the unit commander.

APPEAL PROCESS OVER RELEASE

In principle, every article or videotape prepared by a pool reporter is subject to a one-time censorship procedure in the field, which is conducted by the information officer in consultation with the unit commander.

If a reporter challenges any suggested changes or elisions, the challenge can be adjudicated by the Pentagon and the reporter's editors. In principle, even if the Pentagon rules against publicizing an event, information officers can only appeal to publishers and news directors to suppress it.

The rules can work against print journalism while benefitting television and radio broadcasters. While print journalists must submit written texts of their dispatches to field information officers and commanders for "security review," radio and television reporters often broadcast live without texts, permitting them greater latitude. Television tape, in eight-millimeter format, cannot be reviewed by the videocassette recorder equipment available to information officers in the field.

Varying interpretations of the rules imposed by the Pentagon have virtually blanked out timely publication of some articles that had been cleared by local commanders.

A pool dispatch prepared by The New York Times reported that F-117A radar-evading Stealth bombers launched the war against Iraq with precise laser-guided bombs that destroyed key targets in Baghdad.

SECOND THOUGHTS BY COMMANDER

An Army public information officer cleared the dispatch on the spot for transmission to pool headquarters in Dhahran and then to news organizations themselves.

But more than three hours later, the unit commander had second thoughts about the dispatch, striking out a paragraph and changing words and phrases in others.

To hasten the transmission of the news, The Times reporter agreed to the proposed changes so that American publications and news services could receive it in time for deadlines.

The next day, however, the reporter learned that the entire article had been suppressed by the F-117A unit headquarters in the United States. More than a day after it was written, when it had become stale news, the dispatch was cleared in its original form.

Most reporters are uncomfortable with a news system so completely under military control. The system implemented here has its roots in military dissatisfaction with news coverage of the Vietnam War, which some military officials continue to argue was lost by the news media.

A senior Air Force officer opened his briefing here last week by telling an auditorium filled with reporters: "Let me say up front that I don't like the press. Your presence here can't possibly do me any good, and it can hurt me and my people."

CHAPTER 2

The Role of Censorship in Authoritarian Regimes

Outside of the West, many governments regard their citizens not as active members of society but as a possible threat. In an effort to meet that threat, regimes throughout the world have employed censorship as a means to not only silence dissent but to censor their citizens. The advent of modern technology has simplified what was once a difficult task. With the cooperation of international companies and social media, authoritarian regimes locate and brand political dissidents through their search histories, email and private data.

Stealth Censorship in Venezuela

OPINION | BY DANIEL LANSBERG-RODRÍGUEZ | AUG. 6, 2014

CHICAGO — It's an odd feeling, being silenced. On the Fourth of July, I heard that El Universal, Venezuela's century-old newspaper, and among the oldest in Latin America, had been sold to a recently registered, anonymous Spanish corporation. Against a backdrop of fireworks bursting over Lake Michigan, I sat at my computer and started copying from its website into Word documents two years' worth of weekly opinion columns I had written for the paper. I knew a flood was coming — I had seen it happen before. My laptop would be my pieces' ark.

Sure enough, last week, I received the following notification by email: "Hello and good afternoon, I hope you are well. We're sorry to inform you that, due to editorial restructuring, there has been a series of adjustments and we will no longer be able to publish your work. Many thanks."

The wording was perfect. My articles could no longer be published not because of their quality or anything to do with their content, but by virtue of being mine. Apparently I had called out the government — for mismanaging the electric grid, borrowing recklessly from China, imprisoning political opponents — one too many times.

Dozens of other columnists at the paper received similar notices recently. The contributions of others, including the most celebrated cartoonist in the country, have been censored or edited without notice. Some of those spared have resigned in protest.

El Universal is only the most recent marquee publication to be undone in this fashion since the death of President Hugo Chávez last year. Other casualties include the once-vocal pro-opposition television channel Globovisión and Cadena Capriles, the country's largest newspaper conglomerate (which was previously owned by relatives of the opposition leader Henrique Capriles).

Only one of Venezuela's three big independent newspapers, El Nacional, remains. And for over a year openly critical coverage of the regime has been absent from TV or radio stations.

Censorship is nothing new in Venezuela, but it is taking novel, more covert, forms under Mr. Chávez's lackluster replacement, Nicolás Maduro. Mr. Maduro hasn't made much headway against the problems he inherited from his predecessor: soaring inflation, supply shortages, crumbling infrastructure and criminality. And lacking Mr. Chávez's charisma and talent for masking hard realities with populist promises, he has been leaning hard on the media instead: Censorship has gone from piecemeal to systematic. And like the devil, it is trying to convince the world that it doesn't exist.

Back in 2007, when Mr. Chávez refused to renew the broadcasting license of Radio Caracas Television, which had supported an ephemeral coup against him in 2002, the move was widely condemned, and precipitated paralyzing protests on the streets of Caracas. From that backlash, the government learned the virtues of subtlety. And it discovered that the best way to disguise state suppression of the media was to hand the job over to the free market. Setting socialist rhetoric aside, the government would simply rely on some private-sector leaders — its friends flush with petrodollars — to buy the independent press.

Demise then tends to come in three steps. First, the media outlets are regulated so as to become economically uncompetitive: a newspaper, for example, might be denied a favorable exchange rate for importing printing paper; a broadcaster might regularly be hit with fines on spurious charges of libel or indecency.

Second, once the business starts failing, a dummy corporation, sometimes owned anonymously, mysteriously appears and offers to buy it out, even generously.

Third, despite initially assuring that the editorial line will remain unchanged, the new management soon begins to shed staff, likewise shifting coverage until its message becomes all but indistinguishable from the Panglossian views of the ruling party.

It's a clever strategy. If the government and its supporters are ever accused of censorship, they can counter that a robust percentage of the Venezuelan media industry is independent and privately owned. Even if those particular owners display remarkably little concern for maintaining their customer base or turning a profit.

The end result is an increasingly desolate media landscape: Freedom House recently rated the press in Venezuela as being among the least free in the world, ranking it 171 out of 197 countries, below Singapore, Myanmar and Zimbabwe. (In 2002, it was ranked 86, and in 1992 it was called "free.")

Soon, there may be no free media in Venezuela at all.

For over a century the family-owned El Universal managed to remain independent through military coups, economic depressions, natural disasters, even a socialist revolution. But not under Mr. Maduro. For Mr. Chávez, suppressing the independent media had been a personal thing: He would fixate on a specific outfit he felt had slighted him and stalk it like prey. For Mr. Maduro censorship is state policy — dispassionate, sweeping and unrelenting.

DANIEL LANSBERG-RODRÍGUEZ, a former columnist at El Universal, is a Chicago-based geopolitical-risk consultant.

The New Dictators Rule by Velvet Fist

OPINION | BY SERGEI GURIEV AND DANIEL TREISMAN | MAY 24, 2015

THE STANDARD IMAGE of dictatorship is of a government sustained by violence. In 20th-century totalitarian systems, tyrants like Stalin, Hitler and Mao murdered millions in the name of outlandish ideologies. Strongmen like Mobutu Sese Seko in Zaire left trails of blood.

But in recent decades, a new brand of authoritarian government has evolved that is better adapted to an era of global media, economic interdependence and information technology. The "soft" dictators concentrate power, stifling opposition and eliminating checks and balances, while using hardly any violence.

These illiberal leaders — Alberto K. Fujimori of Peru, Vladimir V. Putin of Russia, Viktor Orban of Hungary, Recep Tayyip Erdogan of Turkey, Mahathir Mohamad of Malaysia and Hugo Chávez of Venezuela — threaten to reshape the world order in their image, replacing principles of freedom and law — albeit imperfectly upheld by Western powers — with cynicism and corruption. The West needs to understand how these regimes work and how to confront them.

Some bloody or ideological regimes remain — as in Syria and North Korea — but the balance has shifted. In 1982, 27 percent of nondemocracies engaged in mass killings. By 2012, only 6 percent did. In the same period, the share of nondemocracies with no elected legislature fell to 15 percent from 31 percent.

This sea change might have started with Lee Kuan Yew of Singapore, who combined parliamentary institutions with strict social control, occasional political arrests and frequent lawsuits to cow the press — but also instituted business-friendly policies that helped fuel astronomical growth. The new autocrats often get to power through reasonably fair elections. Mr. Chávez, for instance, won in 1998 in what international observers called one of the most transparent votes in Venezuela's history.

SÉBASTIEN THIBAULT

Soaring approval ratings are a more cost-effective path to dominance than terror. Mr. Erdogan exploited his popularity to amend the Constitution by referendum and to pack Turkey's Constitutional Court.

The new autocrats use propaganda, censorship and other information-based tricks to inflate their ratings and to convince citizens of their superiority over available alternatives. They peddle an amorphous anti-Western resentment: Mr. Orban mocked Europe's political correctness and declining competitiveness while soliciting European Union development aid.

When their economies do well, such leaders co-opt potential critics with material rewards. In harder times, they use censorship. The new autocrats bribe media owners with advertising contracts, threaten libel suits, and encourage pro-regime investors to purchase critical publications.

They dominate the Internet by blocking access to independent websites, hiring "trolls" to flood comments pages with pro-regime spam, and paying hackers to vandalize opposition online media sites.

The new dictatorships preserve a pocket of democratic opposition to simulate competition. Elections prove the boss's popularity. In Kazakhstan, President Nursultan Nazarbayev was recently re-elected with 97.7 percent of the vote.

Advertising technology that was devised to sell Fords and cans of Pepsi gets reapplied. Mr. Putin hired a top Western public-relations company, Ketchum, to lobby for the Kremlin's interests in the West. Others recruit former Western leaders as consultants — Mr. Nazarbayev, for instance, hired Tony Blair — or donate to their foundations.

Above all, the new autocrats use violence sparingly. This is their key innovation. Hitler took credit for liquidating enemies. Mobutu hanged rivals before large audiences, while Idi Amin of Uganda fed the bodies of victims to crocodiles. Claiming responsibility was part of the strategy: It scared citizens.

The new autocrats are not squeamish — they can viciously repress separatists or club unarmed protesters. But violence reveals the regime's true nature and turns supporters into opponents. Today's dictators carefully deny complicity when opposition activists or journalists are murdered. Take the case of the former Ukrainian president Leonid Kuchma. A tape of him reportedly ordering the abduction of a journalist, Georgy Gongadze, who was later found dead, helped fuel the Orange Revolution of 2004, which brought Mr. Kuchma's rivals to power.

And violence is not just costly — it's unnecessary. Instead, the new authoritarians immobilize political rivals with endless court proceedings, interrogations and other legal formalities. No need to create martyrs when one can defeat opponents by wasting their time. Mr. Putin's agents have begun numerous criminal cases against the opposition leader Aleksei A. Navalny: He has been accused of defrauding a French cosmetics company and stealing wood and interrogated about the killing of an elk.

The West first needs to address its own role in enabling these autocrats. Lobbying for dictators should be considered a serious breach of business ethics. Western democracies should provide objective native-language news broadcasts to counter the propaganda and censorship. And because the information-based dictatorships are susceptible to the pressures of modernization and inevitable economic failings, we need patience.

Besides propaganda, citizens get information by their paychecks — in the Russian idiom, they can choose either "the television or the refrigerator."

SERGEI GURIEV is a professor of economics at Sciences Po, Paris.
DANIEL TREISMAN is a professor of political science at the University of California, Los Angeles.

Egypt Officials Stop Facebook Program for Free Access to Internet

BY KAREEM FAHIM | DEC. 30, 2015

CAIRO — A program that provided more than three million Egyptians with free access to Internet services was abruptly shut down on Wednesday, according to Facebook, the social media company that provided the program in cooperation with an Egyptian cellphone company.

The reasons for the suspension were not immediately clear. A person familiar with the program, called Free Basics, which provides free access to text-only versions of Facebook and other services, said the Egyptian government had ordered it closed down. Reuters quoted an Egyptian telecommunications official as saying that Etisalat, the cellphone company that carried the services, had been granted a two-month permit for Free Basics that had expired on Wednesday.

The suspension comes as the government of President Abdel Fattah El-Sisi has intensified its efforts to thwart any possible protests on Jan. 25, the fifth anniversary of the Arab Spring uprising that toppled President Hosni Mubarak. Social media had played a critical role in the 2011 revolt, including Facebook, which organizers used to mobilize the massive demonstrations that ultimately led to the fall of Mr. Mubarak.

The government banned any unauthorized protests more than two years ago. In recent days, the authorities have arrested young anti-government dissidents affiliated with the anti-Mubarak uprising, and raided cultural organizations that were gathering places for young activists.

In a statement, Facebook said the company was "disappointed that Free Basics will no longer be available in Egypt," and said it hoped "to resolve this situation soon."

The program, which started in Egypt in October, was part of Facebook's ambitious and disputed plan to bring Internet service to billions of people in developing countries. In its statement, Facebook said that of the more than three million Egyptians who had signed up, more than one million "were previously unconnected" to the Internet.

Free Basics has drawn criticism, including for providing a limited service with selected partners rather than unrestricted Internet access, and for violating net neutrality, which calls for all Internet services to be treated equally by telecommunications carriers.

Facebook's chief executive, Mark Zuckerberg, has mounted an aggressive campaign to defend Free Basics, including running full-page newspaper ads and writing an opinion piece published in The Times of India on Monday that asked, "Who could possibly be against this?"

The program, which operates in more than two dozen countries, offers cellphone users free access to a limited set of Internet services including Facebook's social network and messaging services, news, health and job information.

Facebook argues that the program introduces the poor to the Internet and that many become paying customers for broader access to the Internet.

Last week, regulators in India ordered the suspension of the program after Reliance Communications, Facebook's partner there, failed to provide information on the service before a planned expansion.

VINDU GOEL contributed reporting from San Francisco.

How Egypt Crowdsources Censorship

OPINION | BY YASMINE EL RASHIDI | DEC. 8, 2018

It's not just the government suppressing free expression, it's our neighbors — and ourselves.

Ms. El Rashidi is a longtime resident of Cairo.

CAIRO — To write in Egypt and about Egypt has long meant being under the scrutiny of an authoritarian state — starting in the 1950s with President Gamal Abdel Nasser, who nationalized the press, and extending to the present. If you didn't approve of the government's activities, your only option, you quickly learned, was to be noncommittal.

My first encounter with the red lines of authority was in the early 2000s, as a young writer at a weekly paper in Cairo. One day my editor, a well-respected journalist who stood apart from his submissive state-appointed colleagues for his outspokenness and professional rigor, called me into his office after an editorial meeting. I had proposed to write about an impending gas deal with Israel. He was apologetic but clear: There would be no talk of the gas deal.

There was an official blackout on coverage of Egypt's relations with Israel. Border issues were off-limits. So was heavy metal music, thought to be a pact with the devil. Particular turns of phrase also were no-nos: "iron-fisted," for example, when used to describe the president, since any criticism of him could land you in jail. I quickly learned the ropes and the bounds, and I inadvertently, not conscious of the act itself, learned to self-censor, too.

This, in many ways, was the beginning of what would become a growing space of silence in my writing life, which slowly extended beyond politics. Over the years, I developed a habit of sidestepping or writing in innuendo anything that I thought might be culturally offensive, exposing, taboo.

GOLDEN COSMOS

In the fall of 2010, the year before the revolution that ousted President Hosni Mubarak, I was part of a small team of writers and editors that founded the online news site Ahram Online. It was partly funded by the state and under the umbrella of the government daily Al Ahram. But our editor, Hani Shukrallah, was a liberal and a leftist — a fierce defender of press freedoms and human rights, who encouraged us to push boundaries. After that year's particularly contentious parliamentary election, during which Mr. Mubarak's ruling National Democratic Party hired thugs to beat up dissident candidates, we ran an article with the headline "Blow by Blow Account." Mr. Shukrallah almost immediately got a phone call from the chairman of Al Ahram.

He came out of his office and grudgingly told us that the headline had to go. We changed it to "Minute by Minute Account." We also chopped off the last paragraph of an article I was writing because it mentioned the president's younger son, Gamal, who was angling for power in a standoff with the army. This type of censorship, slight in many ways, severe in others, had become a mode of survival; one picked one's battles.

Still, it was only for a fleeting moment in 2011, in the early days of the uprising — before any clear division between factions had become apparent — that my notebook felt like a liability: I was stopped several times on the street by police officers who were suspicious of my note-taking and interrogated me about my affiliation and intentions.

In all my years of writing, it had always been clear what could and what couldn't be addressed, even when the difference between those things shifted as the political story changed. There was still a margin for challenging the status quo, to subtly suggest what could not be said — that was mostly a matter of timing and venue. Writing in English, one had more leeway. Sometimes journalists were jailed and people disappeared, but such perils didn't loom over the everyday or anyone I personally knew.

The present, in this broader historical context, feels novel. In the space of a single day in April, three journalists were detained. Over the whole year, the number is thought to be 38. Others have disappeared. The crackdown now also extends beyond journalists, to anyone with a voice: actresses, comedians, satirists, bloggers, poets, singers, photographers and researchers.

The journalist and novelist Ahmed Naji was sentenced to two years in prison because of sexually explicit scenes from his novel that were published in a magazine. The poet Fatima Naoot was sentenced to three years in prison after she wrote a Facebook post calling the slaughter of sheep during the Muslim festival of Eid al-Adha "the most horrible massacre committed by humans."

This summer, Galal el-Beheiry was also sentenced to a three-year term, for the title of his anthology of poems, which plays on a phrase critical of the military. The Egyptian singer Shyma was imprisoned in January for making a suggestive music video involving a banana; another singer was also jailed — for joking about the cleanliness of the

Nile's waters. This week, an actress was handed a trial date for wearing to the Cairo International Film Festival a fishnet dress revealing her legs.

Many of these works, which earned their creators charges of "blasphemy," "offending public morals," "inciting debauchery" or "contempt of religion," were reported to the prosecutor's office by fellow citizens who questioned their morality. The laws are vague enough to act as a catchall. The crusade to silence words, images and thoughts is both opaque and arbitrary. What may well escape the state censor might still offend a neighbor — partly because the government has encouraged citizens to report fake news and "forces of evil."

For decades under past presidents, the conservative current in Egyptian society had been kept in check. But the government of Abdel Fattah el-Sisi, keen to show itself as no less religious than the Islamist leadership it ousted, has allowed the righteous to speak up. Censorship, too, can be crowdsourced.

Writing an essay on Egypt for The New York Review of Books some months ago, I spent many hours over many days debating the inclusion of certain words. "Heteronormative" might not be understood; "heterosexual" might be misinterpreted. Or perhaps they were both too fraught, an affront to some people's morals, simply for intimating the acceptance of other lifestyles. After debating the issue with friends, I scratched the sentence altogether. I went through a similar process recently in editing the Arabic edition of my novel, guided by a publisher well versed in the morphing standards of acceptability.

Today, the risks exist regardless of who you are, what platform you write or speak for, what language you choose to use. The bounds of right and wrong now extend beyond the parameters of a political system, to what is deemed to be moral for the culture and conscientious for the nation. This is a moment of crisis, when new forms of expression and resistance must emerge.

A question occupies me today: How to silence the censor inside me when faced with a growing sense of foreboding, even at times fear? How to invent, from this moment and this pressure, something radical, bound-breaking, new?

YASMINE EL RASHIDI is the author of "The Battle for Egypt: Dispatches from the Revolution" and "Chronicle of a Last Summer: A Novel of Egypt," and a contributing opinion writer.

Turks Click Away, but Wikipedia Is Gone

BY PATRICK KINGSLEY | JUNE 10, 2017

ISTANBUL — Baris Dede, a game design student, had a question: How easily did Viking longboats glide through the water? Dilara Diner, a psychologist, wanted to double-check a symptom of hysteria.

But these Turks were not able to quickly find out what they wanted. Since late April the Turkish government has blocked one of the world's go-to sources of online information, Wikipedia.

After Wikipedia refused to remove unflattering references to Turkey's relationship with Syrian militants and state-sponsored terrorists, officials simply banned the whole site.

Several weeks into the ban, some Turks are still struggling to remove Wikipedia searches from their muscle memory.

Yaman Akdeniz, a law professor, turned by habit to Wikipedia to find out when the latest "House of Cards" season was released.

"You forget that it's blocked, and then you click on it and then — boomph, nothing: You realize you can't access it," said Professor Akdeniz, describing his personal form of digital whiplash. Many people didn't realize until after it was blocked, he said, that Wikipedia "was so much a part of our lives."

Mr. Dede said he mourned the loss of "part of your memory." Even in his academic world, where Wikipedia is sometimes scorned, the website was secretly seen as a good starting place for research, he said.

But beyond the problems it has created for the curious, Turkey's Wikipedia ban is a reminder of something darker, government critics say: a wholesale crackdown on free expression and access to information, amid wider oppression of most forms of opposition.

Wikipedia is just one of 127,000 websites blocked in Turkey, estimated Professor Akdeniz, who has led legal challenges against the

Wikipedia ban and other web restrictions. An additional 95,000 pages, like social media accounts, blog posts and articles, are blocked on websites that are not otherwise restricted, Mr. Akdeniz said.

Some of these sites are pornographic. But many contain information and reporting that the government finds embarrassing. Sendika, an independent news outlet, is now on the 45th iteration of its website. The previous 44 were blocked.

For web activists in Turkey, Wikipedia is simply the latest victim of a wave of online censorship that grew steadily from 2015 onward and then surged significantly after last year's failed coup.

The coup attempt gave President Recep Tayyip Erdogan the political cover to expand a crackdown on his opponents, including in the traditional news media. Since the coup, 190 news organizations have been banned and at least 120 journalists jailed.

"The international community noticed this issue by reference to the Wikipedia block, but it's not a new thing from our point of view," Mr. Akdeniz said. "Critical media is under stress on a daily basis — and what made that visible is the Wikipedia ban."

For students, the ban could not have come at a worse time: just as they were knuckling down for exams.

"It's a big obstacle," said Ege, a 17-year-old high school student, whose surname has been withheld at the wishes of his headmaster. "Wikipedia is the source of the sources — you can find everything there."

While studying Jean Anouilh's French adaptation of a Greek tragedy, "Antigone," Ege's friends had wanted to know more about the heroine's father: the mythical King Oedipus, who mistakenly married his mother.

"The Oedipus bloodline, what he did, the curse that was put on his family," Ege's classmate Yusuf said. "Reaching that information wasn't exactly easy."

Wikipedia use has fallen by 85 percent in Turkey since April, but some have managed to circumvent the ban with a VPN, or virtual private network, a tool that helps web users gain access to blocked websites.

According to GlobalWebIndex, a group that researches worldwide internet activity, Turkey has the third-highest VPN prevalence in the world. More than 45 percent of Turks ages 16 to 64 who have web access used a VPN in the first quarter of 2017, and the practice has become second nature even for some beginners.

"My mom learned to send an email two years ago," Mr. Dede said. "The next thing, she's learning how to access a VPN."

But VPN use comes with an unwelcome side effect. Because Wikipedia does not allow VPN users to edit articles, Turks are unable to correct or update information posted on the site or write new articles.

"Turkey has lost its voice online because of its inability to edit Wikipedia," said Alp Toker, a co-founder of Turkey Blocks, a group that tracks Turkish internet censorship.

In addition, some VPNs are also banned. Those that remain are often slow, particularly on cellphones, so using one is sometimes not worth the hassle.

As a result, some students are getting desperate about their final exams.

"Dear President of the Republic, the Leader, open up Wikipedia at least until the end of the finals week," one wrote on Twitter. "President, I am overwhelmed, hear me out."

Erdogan's Next Target as He Restricts Turkey's Democracy: The Internet

BY CARLOTTA GALL | MARCH 4, 2018

ISTANBUL — Having already brought Turkey's mainstream media to heel, and made considerable headway in rolling back Turkish democracy, the government of President Recep Tayyip Erdogan has set its sights on a seemingly innocuous target: a satellite television preacher named Adnan Oktar.

For seven years, with an unholy blend of the racy and the religious, Mr. Oktar has presented his show daily via satellite, cable and the internet, where he expounds on Islamic creationism, peace and love, often to a studio audience of women in miniskirts and plunging necklines.

Religious conservatives in the government now say they want to shut him down. But critics say that Mr. Oktar has become a convenient trigger for the government to pursue wide-reaching restrictions on internet content and broadcasters.

The real aim, they say, besides enforcing moral standards on the likes of Mr. Oktar, is to close off a final refuge for the news media and the political opposition as the government widens an already formidable crackdown on dissent.

Just three days after the government announced its campaign against Mr. Oktar, it introduced an expansive set of new internet restrictions that would affect millions of Turks who use the internet and social media.

"With Master Adnan as an excuse, extensive censorship coming for internet media," one news website headline warned.

The draft law has passed the parliamentary commission stage, and may go to a vote next week, legislators say.

Even before it is passed, outside authorities are raising alarms. Harlem Désir, representative on freedom of the media at the Organization for Security and Cooperation in Europe, urged legislators to revise the bill, saying it restricted pluralism online and could be incompatible with international conventions.

But a creeping control of the media has been a persistent feature of Mr. Erdogan's 15 years in power. He has used every legal means, as well as extraordinary emergency powers since a failed coup in 2016, to steadily turn Turkey into an authoritarian system under his thumb.

As Mr. Erdogan plans to run in an election for a presidency with newly enhanced powers, which may come this year, the new media law would put yet another heavy finger on the scale in his favor. It would allow him to mute whatever opposition voices have not already been silenced.

"It is just about control," said Kerem Altiparmak, a human rights and media lawyer. "Considering what has been happening in Turkey, I have no doubt this is a hegemonic power, controlling newspapers, TV and the judiciary, that is now out to control the internet sector."

The irony is that Mr. Erdogan is responsible for the economic progress that has made Turkey a largely middle-class country and allowed many to be educated and able to afford cellphones and the internet.

A former businessman and mayor of Istanbul, Mr. Erdogan began his transformation of Turkey by building on the early, enormous popularity he gained with social programs that offered health care and pensions to all, and infrastructure projects that eased housing and transportation strains.

Initially, he oversaw democratic reforms as part of Turkey's bid for European Union membership. But as Mr. Erdogan notched up electoral successes, he not only undermined his opponents but he also turned on various allies who had helped him rise to power.

His first target was Turkey's once powerful military, which he emasculated with a series of arrests and high-profile trials that was completed in 2013.

Later, he turned against former allies within the Islamist movement, followers of the preacher Fethullah Gulen, who lives in the United States. They had led the campaign to dismantle the military and were demanding a greater share of power.

In 2013, Mr. Erdogan closed down the network of university-preparatory schools run by Mr. Gulen, cutting into a major source of finance and influence for his movement.

When supporters of Mr. Gulen attempted a coup in the summer of 2016, Mr. Erdogan answered with his nationwide crackdown, which is drawing increasing rebuke in Europe.

So far, Mr. Erdogan has detained more than 60,000 people accused of being Gulen followers and purged or suspended 150,000 government employees. He also used the opportunity to round up academics, journalists and political opponents.

The purges hastened the trend under Mr. Erdogan's leadership of placing loyalists in government and public institutions. The police, judiciary and even universities have by now been transformed.

In fact, virtually all the levers of power now belong to Mr. Erdogan, including much of the news media.

The government tamed the largest and most powerful media companies by imposing huge tax fines on them and forcing them to sell off assets, and pushing loyal businessmen to take over publications and television channels.

After the 2016 coup, 150 media outlets were closed down, and journalists were imprisoned at a pace that left Turkey second only to China, a much larger country, for the numbers jailed.

In 2002, when Mr. Erdogan became prime minister, pro-government businesses owned fewer than a quarter of Turkish media outlets, according to "The New Sultan: Erdogan and the Crisis of Modern Turkey," by Soner Cagaptay, director of the Turkish research program at The Washington Institute.

By 2011, they owned about 50 percent, and by 2017 most of the mainstream media outlets were in their hands. Censors control content in government media offices, and private media outlets are issued strict guidelines.

"Erdogan can successfully edit out reality," Mr. Cagaptay said in an interview.

The co-opting of the mainstream media has helped push Turks, especially the young and middle class, to the internet, which is delivering popular alternatives to a growing audience.

Besides a growing number of entertainment providers, including Netflix, and the Turkish equivalents Puhu TV and BluTV, there are several lively independent internet news outlets that publish through social media platforms and podcasts.

All of them could be targeted under an article slipped into the innocuous-sounding bill under consideration — "Tax Law and the Law to Change Some Laws and Decrees."

As drafted it would force any outlets broadcasting via the internet to be licensed. It would also give the watchdog Radio and Television Supreme Council powers to halt live-streaming and fine companies over content.

Ahmet Arslan, minister for transportation and communication, who denies there is censorship in Turkey, defended the bill before journalists at an event celebrating Secure Internet Day.

"We have to take measures about radio and television broadcasts if there is a wrongdoing about national security, and ethical values of the country," Mr. Arslan said.

"Our aim is to bring a legal regulation, and prevent mistakes," he added. "It is certainly not to intervene against any correct broadcasting, any work that is done in harmony with our values."

The government already imposes restrictions on television shows, making channels edit out curses and blur cigarettes and alcohol. Shows viewed via the internet have so far escaped such controls.

"If there is any wrongdoing, there should of course be an intervention," Mr. Arslan concluded. "This is the aim of the regulation."

But Mr. Altiparmak, who is also a lecturer in law at the University of Ankara, said that while it was necessary to license television channels, because television frequencies were limited, the internet was limitless and so licensing was not necessary in the same way.

Instead, the bill would merely allow the government to block any outlet it dislikes by refusing a license without having to prove grounds of national security or ethics.

"The first thing is a judge will be able to block a website without having to show a reason," he said. "Second they can bring sanctions against TV stations and fines on internet TV."

The Turkish telecommunications regulatory authority, BTK, already regulates internet providers, removing content and blocking websites that it disapproves of.

Wikipedia has been blocked for months, pro-Kurdish news sites are frequently closed down, and a leftist website Sendika.org has renamed itself 62 times to get around government blocks.

Indeed, the scale of the government crackdown has instilled such fear and suspicion in Turkey that many intellectuals and journalists have fled the country.

In the first weeks of 2018, as Turkey began a military operation against Kurdish militants in the northern Syrian enclave of Afrin, the police detained more than 600 people for opposing the intervention on social media or for taking part in protests.

Garo Paylan, a member of Parliament for the pro-Kurdish People's Democratic Party and a member of the commission studying the bill, warned that the government intended to curb the internet the same way it had constrained television and newspapers.

"Any kind of broadcast over social media can be included, which means millions of people won't be able to broadcast," he said in a telephone interview.

"Only supporters will be able to get a license," he added. "And it would cost an amount. Many people would hold back from applying."

The government could take action against anyone broadcasting without a license, although Hamit Ersoy, a member of Radio and Television Supreme Council, said the bill was aimed at online on-demand broadcasting and not social media, in comments to the Anadolu news agency.

Mr. Paylan's predominantly Kurdish party has especially suffered. Nine lawmakers are in jail, including the leader of the party, who was accused of terrorism. The party is effectively banned from all mainstream media.

Its legislators now broadcast parliamentary news to their followers via Facebook's Periscope. Now those broadcasts could be stopped as well, Mr. Paylan said.

"If enacted, we will see the same situation for internet that the press and television fell into," he said. "And this will detach us from the rest of the world more."

Reuters Publishes Account of Myanmar Massacre After Journalists' Arrests

BY RICHARD C. PADDOCK | FEB. 10, 2018

BANGKOK — The news agency Reuters has published a detailed investigation into the massacre of 10 Rohingya men by Myanmar soldiers and villagers, saying that the work led the Myanmar authorities to arrest two of its reporters.

The article, which was published on Friday, describes how soldiers and Buddhist villagers carried out the killings in September and buried the victims in a single grave. Based on eyewitness accounts, it includes photographs of the Rohingya men tied up and kneeling before their execution, and images after their deaths.

Pictures taken later show what appear to be human bone fragments at the site of the mass grave.

Two of the four journalists who worked on the report, U Wa Lone and U Kyaw Soe Oo, were arrested in December and face trial on charges of violating Myanmar's colonial-era Official Secrets Act. They have been denied bail and face up to 14 years in prison.

The massacre described in the Reuters report occurred during a wave of attacks on the Rohingya Muslim minority in Rakhine State last year that Secretary of State Rex W. Tillerson said "constitutes ethnic cleansing."

At least 6,700 Rohingya met violent deaths, including 730 children younger than 5, and hundreds of villages were destroyed as the military and Buddhist residents of the area sought revenge for deadly attacks on police posts by Rohingya insurgents.

About 700,000 Rohingya have fled across the border into Bangladesh to escape the violence.

In its 4,500-word article, Reuters documented the killings of the 10

Rohingya men in Inn Din village, about 30 miles north of Sittwe, the capital of Rakhine State.

The report identified the victims by name and described them as fishermen, shopkeepers and an Islamic teacher. Two were high school students. They ranged in age from 17 to 45.

At least two of the men were hacked to death by Buddhist villagers, and the rest were shot by Myanmar troops, Reuters reported, citing eyewitnesses who are Buddhist.

"One grave for 10 people," said U Soe Chay, 55, a retired soldier who told Reuters that he had helped to dig the grave and saw the killings. The soldiers shot each man two or three times, he said, but not all died immediately.

"When they were being buried, some were still making noises," Reuters quoted him as saying. "Others were already dead."

In January, the military confirmed that 10 Rohingya men were killed in Inn Din by villagers and soldiers. It said the men were terrorists who had attacked security forces, and that the soldiers had decided to kill them because intense fighting made it impossible to keep them in custody. The army said it would take action against those involved.

U Zaw Htay, a government spokesman, told Reuters, "We are not denying the allegations about violations of human rights."

He added, "If we found the evidence is true and the violations are there, we will take the necessary action according to our existing law."

Reuters said its report was based on scores of interviews with Rakhine Buddhist villagers, soldiers, paramilitary police officers, Rohingya Muslims and local administrators.

The villagers told Reuters that the military and the paramilitary police had organized Buddhist residents of Inn Din and at least two other villages to set fire to Rohingya homes, and that Buddhist villagers had participated in the killings of Rohingya in the area.

The government has accused Rohingya insurgents of burning the homes themselves.

Citing unidentified sources, the report said that an order to clear Inn Din had been passed down the military chain of command and that security forces wore civilian clothes to avoid being detected during raids.

Members of the paramilitary police looted Rohingya property, including motorcycles and cows, some of which were later taken by the military, Reuters reported.

None of the 6,000 Rohingya who once lived in Inn Din were still there by October.

The photographs of the 10 victims before and after the killings were provided by a Buddhist village elder who said he did not want to see the events repeated.

Mr. Wa Lone and Mr. Kyaw Soe Oo, the two journalists being held by the Myanmar authorities, had done extensive reporting on the massacre before they were arrested on Dec. 12. Reuters said Mr. Wa Lone had taken some photographs of the mass grave.

Human rights groups have accused the police of entrapping the two journalists by handing them documents. One relative said the two men had been seized so quickly that they did not have a chance to examine the documents.

Why Are So Many Democracies Breaking Down?

OPINION | BY MICHAEL ALBERTUS AND VICTOR MENALDO | MAY 8, 2018

Mr. Albertus and Mr. Menaldo are the authors of "Authoritarianism and the Elite Origins of Democracy."

ITALY, POLAND, HUNGARY and even Spain: European democracy is in shambles. Critical threats to democracy have also surfaced in countries like Turkey, Brazil and the Philippines. Under President Trump's "America First" orientation, leaders with authoritarian tendencies in places as disparate as Egypt, Honduras, Russia and Venezuela have trampled their political opponents without concern for anything more harmful than a tongue lashing from the United States.

Why do democracies backslide toward authoritarianism? Many scholars point to the worrisome erosion of democratic norms rooted in a social consensus about the rules of the game and civility toward fellow citizens.

But this erosion of democratic norms is ultimately driven by deeper factors. In many democracies, the roots of breakdown reside in democratic constitutions themselves.

Over two-thirds of countries that have transitioned to democracy since World War II have done so under constitutions written by the outgoing authoritarian regime. Prominent examples include Argentina, Chile, Kenya, Mexico, Nigeria, South Africa and South Korea. Even some of the world's early democracies, such as the Netherlands and Sweden, were marred by deep authoritarian legacies. Democratic institutions are frequently designed by the outgoing authoritarian regime to safeguard incumbent elites from the rule of law and give them a leg up in politics and economic competition after democratization.

The constitutional tools that outgoing authoritarian elites use to accomplish these ends include factors like electoral system design,

Daw Aung San Suu Kyi met with Senior Gen. Min Aung Hlaing after a meeting in 2015.

legislative appointments, federalism, legal immunities, the role of the military in politics and constitutional tribunal design. In short, with the allocation of power and privilege, and the lived experiences of citizens, democracy often does not restart the political game after displacing authoritarianism.

Furthermore, barriers to changing the social contract in countries that inherit constitutions from a previous authoritarian regime are steep. These constitutions often contain provisions requiring supermajority thresholds for change. And elites from the authoritarian past who benefit from these constitutions utilize their power to pass policies that further entrench their privileges.

Myanmar is a prime example of how outgoing authoritarian regimes can game democracy in their favor. The 2015 elections that brought Daw Aung San Suu Kyi and the National League for Democracy to power were conducted within the framework of the 2008 constitution that the military wrote. Before handing over power, the military-dominated legislature passed a flurry of legislation that included promises of amnesty to military generals who have been accused of human rights abuses, a generous pension plan for departing lawmakers, lucrative business contracts slated to benefit outgoing generals and other elites and the transfer of manufacturing plants from the ministry of industry to the ministry of defense. And, critically, the constitution awards the military 25 percent of seats in parliament — precisely the figure needed to block constitutional reform. Its position remains so powerful that many observers wonder whether Ms. Aung San Suu Kyi and the N.L.D., despite winning the 2015 elections in a landslide, are now held hostage by the military's brutal purging of Myanmar's Rohingya population.

A critical consequence of the trend that new democracies tend to have their social contracts written by outgoing dictators is that while these democracies may be formed of the people, they do not function by or for the people. Citizens may be free from some of the worst abuses of authoritarianism, such as blanket censorship and outright repression, but they are not important players in determining public policy. In this way, democracy is a sort of purgatory in which they wander — sometimes for decades — with little capacity to determine its direction.

This is a recipe for discontent with democracy. Major crises like a severe economic recession can provide the tinder for citizen disaffection to crystallize into rage and inciting voters to throw out traditional political parties en masse. This discontent can ultimately lead to democratic demise, as inexperienced new political actors appeal to demagogy and dismantle longstanding institutions without building a more solidly democratic foundation.

Consider Turkey, where President Recep Tayyip Erdogan has used bluster and constitutional reform to gut the checks and balances and military vetoes that previously hemmed in civilian politicians. The 1982 authoritarian constitution that guided Turkey's 1983 transition to democracy created a constitutional court with the ability to ban political parties like Communists and overtly religious parties. The military maintained autonomy over its budget and decision-making. Perhaps most egregiously, the top military brass and their collaborators made sure there was a series of clauses and articles that granted them immunity from prosecution for any crimes during the authoritarian era. A result was that the military and their allies continued to enjoy economic privileges, like retaining ownership of key industries, while avoiding prosecution for human rights abuses.

In 1987, however, a major amendment to Turkey's 1983 constitution lifted a ban on some outlawed opposition parties. This paved the way for the later rise of new parties like the Justice and Development Party, which, since the early 2000s, in the wake of a major economic crisis, has dominated Turkish politics. Indeed, under the J.D.P. banner, Mr. Erdogan was able to exploit the military's reputation for impunity, as well as the dissatisfaction of clerics and conservative citizens in the Anatolian heartland with the ironclad separation of church and state imposed by the constitution and enforced by the military.

His populist economic policies have been wedded to a protracted campaign to consolidate the power of the executive branch, weaken the military (including jailing officers), empower Islamists, enervate individual liberties and the judiciary, and ultimately replace Turkey's holdover constitution with his own. He achieved that much in 2017 after a popular referendum approved 18 amendments to the constitution, which transformed Turkey into a presidential system in which the executive exercises outsize power, including the ability to appoint the majority of judges and prosecutors.

Democratic erosion has followed a similar pattern in other countries as well. Hungary's ever more authoritarian prime minister, Victor Orban, leveraged popular discontent with the country's Communist-written constitution to renovate Hungarian political institutions with a new constitution in 2011. Mr. Orban's reforms have hobbled the judiciary and cleared the way for his political party, Fidesz, to trample its opponents.

Fortunately, elite-biased democracies can successfully reform their social contracts over time to become more egalitarian and representative of average citizens rather than sliding back into dictatorship. It is not easy or common.

But if it is to be done, it tends to occur in the wake of these very same major crises or economic shocks. Mass citizen mobilization, when married to the material support of a faction of disaffected or disadvantaged elites, can succeed in amending or entirely rewriting democratic constitutions to eliminate the worst distortions to representation.

But this requires patience, magnanimous leadership and citizen faith in the promise of what democracy can deliver — all of which seem to be running increasingly short.

MICHAEL ALBERTUS, an assistant professor of political science at the University of Chicago, and **VICTOR MENALDO**, an associate professor of political science at the University of Washington, are the authors of "Authoritarianism and the Elite Origins of Democracy."

The Website That Shows How a Free Press Can Die

BY PATRICK KINGSLEY AND BENJAMIN NOVAK | NOV. 24, 2018

BUDAPEST — Hungary's leading news website, Origo, had a juicy scoop: A top aide to the far-right prime minister, Viktor Orban, had used state money to pay for sizable but unexplained expenses during secret foreign trips. The story embarrassed Mr. Orban and was a reminder that his country still had an independent press.

But that was in 2014. Today, Origo is one of the prime minister's most dutiful media boosters, parroting his attacks on migrants and on George Soros, the Hungarian-American philanthropist demonized by the far right on both sides of the Atlantic.

And if Origo once dug into Mr. Orban's government, it now pounces on his political opponents.

"Let's look at the affairs of Laszlo Botka!" a headline blared this month in a salacious take on the only mayor of a major Hungarian city not aligned with Mr. Orban's party, Fidesz. "Serious scandals, mysteries surround the socialist mayor of Szeged."

If little known outside Hungary, Origo is now a cautionary tale for an age in which democratic norms and freedom of expression are being challenged globally — and President Trump and other leaders have intensified attacks on the free press.

In many ways, Hungary has foreshadowed the democratic backsliding now evident in different corners of the world. Since winning power in 2010, Mr. Orban has steadily eroded institutional checks and balances, especially the independent media. His government now oversees state-owned news outlets, while his allies control most of the country's private media sources, creating a virtual echo chamber for Mr. Orban's far right, anti-immigrant views.

The story of Origo's transformation from independent news source to government cheerleader offers a blueprint of how Mr. Orban and his allies pulled this off. Rather than a sudden and blatant power grab, the effort was subtle but determined, using a quiet pressure campaign.

Origo's editors were never imprisoned and its reporters were never beaten up. But in secret meetings — including a pivotal one in Vienna — the website's original owner, a German-owned telecommunications company, relented. The company, Magyar Telekom, first tried self-censorship. Then it sought a nonpartisan buyer.

But, ultimately, Origo went to the family of Mr. Orban's former finance minister.

"When Orban came to power in 2010, his aim was to eliminate the media's role as a check on government," said Attila Mong, a former public radio anchor and a critic of Mr. Orban. "Orban wanted to introduce a regime which keeps the facade of democratic institutions but is not operated in a democratic manner — and a free press doesn't fit into that picture."

On the surface, Hungary's democratic institutions seem to be operating normally. The judiciary is nominally independent. Elections are held. Newsstands are stacked with dozens of private publications.

"We would never sink so low," Mr. Orban said in a September speech, "as to silence those with whom we disagree."

But below the surface, the system has been degraded. The Constitutional Court is stacked with judges appointed by Fidesz. The judiciary and the prosecution service are headed by two of Mr. Orban's oldest supporters. Both the electoral system and the electoral map have been altered to favor Mr. Orban's party.

Other than a handful of mainly online outlets, the Hungarian media has been either silent about or supportive of these moves.

According to Freedom House's press freedom index, Hungary's media was judged the 87th freest in the world in 2017, down from joint 40th in 2010, when Mr. Orban entered office.

The index now labels Hungarian media as only "partly free," while Hungary's wider political system, once classified as a "consolidated democracy," has been downgraded to "semi-consolidated democracy."

And the fate of Origo, Mr. Mong said, is "very symbolic" of that transition.

A SECRET MEETING

In 2013, Origo was Hungary's most-read news website, renowned for its hard-nosed investigations into the likes of Lajos Simicska, a friend of Mr. Orban who had long financed his party.

By then, Mr. Orban's appointees controlled the state media, as well as Hungary's two main media regulators. He had given regulators more power to fine and punish independent news outlets, or to drive them off air, yet Origo did not seem cowed.

The site had been created in the late 1990s by Magyar Telekom, the country's leading telecoms company, to lure subscribers to its fledgling internet service. Over time, though, Origo evolved into a journalistic force with its own identity.

But as Origo thrived, its parent company faced challenges.

Since the start of the cellphone era, Magyar Telekom had been Hungary's leading telecommunications company. When Deutsche Telekom, the German telecoms giant that also owns T-Mobile, bought a majority stake in the company in 2005, Magyar Telekom was considered a marquee purchase.

But things changed with Mr. Orban's election in 2010. He levied an "emergency" tax on the telecoms sector, in a bid to reduce government debt after the global financial crisis. The tax was also seen as part of a wider backlash against foreign firms that had bought up large sections of the Hungarian economy after the fall of communism.

For Magyar Telekom, it meant an additional $100 million tax bill. Company executives feared more bad news in 2013, when Mr. Orban's government was due to renew its frequency licenses. Ahead of a September deadline, negotiations would determine how much of the market would be assigned to Telekom, and at what price.

The talks were not going well. Months before the deadline, René Obermann, Deutsche Telekom's chief executive, became embroiled in a shouting match with Mr. Orban at a private meeting in Germany, two people briefed on the exchange said.

Throughout the year, Magyar Telekom executives met with Janos Lazar, Mr. Orban's second-in-command, to negotiate the license renewal and a multimillion-dollar contract to install broadband internet throughout rural Hungary. Initially, Origo was not a topic of discussion.

But that changed in the early summer at a secret meeting in Vienna between Mr. Lazar and two senior company executives, according to three people with knowledge of the discussion. Mr. Lazar said that Origo's journalists had historically struggled to grasp the government's perspective on certain matters and proposed a remedy: a secret line of communication between Origo's editors and the highest levels of government.

Mr. Lazar was careful not to frame the request as a quid pro quo for new licenses, or as a form of censorship. But the Magyar Telekom executives took it seriously.

By autumn, Origo had signed a contract with a media consultancy run by Attila Varhegyi, the former director of Mr. Orban's party. As a consultant, Mr. Varhegyi had played a major role in turning Hungarian state media into a mouthpiece for Mr. Orban and now his attention had pivoted to the private sector.

Under the deal, Mr. Varhegyi's firm could call Origo's editor with suggestions about coverage.

That same month, the government extended its license agreements with the country's three mobile telephone operators.

Magyar Telekom was awarded the biggest share.

Both Magyar Telekom and its parent company declined to comment on the Vienna meeting and Mr. Varhegyi. But in a general statement, Magyar Telekom said: "Dialogue between the government in office and the management of Magyar Telekom is a matter of fact, but its aim has never been to limit publicity or the freedom of press."

Mr. Varhegyi and Mr. Lazar turned down several interview requests and ignored requests for comment.

AN EDITOR IS FIRED

Outraged, Origo's editor in chief resigned, refusing to participate in the deal. But his replacement, Gergo Saling, appeared undaunted.

By January 2014, one member of Mr. Saling's team had even begun an investigation into Mr. Lazar's foreign travel expenses. Requests by Mr. Varhegyi's firm to slow the project down were ignored.

But Mr. Saling was living on borrowed time.

The investigation was embarrassing to Magyar Telekom: Mr. Lazar had overseen the company's license renewal and discussions were still underway over the contract to install broadband in the countryside.

Mr. Lazar complained about the story in a meeting with two Magyar Telekom executives in February 2014, according to two people with knowledge of the discussion, and his disapproval was quickly relayed to Origo's management. It was one of several attempts by Magyar Telekom management, and Mr. Varhegyi's firm, to sway the investigation, both before and after the broadband deal was announced later that month, according to four people familiar with the controversy.

Undeterred, Origo continued to scrutinize Mr. Lazar's travel. Origo eventually began court proceedings to request specific travel records, and published several embarrassing stories about the minister's movements.

But by the start of summer, Mr. Saling's superiors had run out of patience. Mr. Orban had won re-election in April. Mr. Saling was fired in early June, nominally by mutual agreement.

The decision was ultimately made by Miklos Vaszily, Origo's chief executive. But it came only after months of pressure on Mr. Vaszily from Magyar Telekom's management and Mr. Varhegyi's firm, according to three people at the company.

In protest, several of Origo's best reporters resigned.

For Magyar Telekom, Origo had become a public relations liability and a political hindrance, and executives wanted to sell.

FLUSH WITH GOVERNMENT CASH

Throughout 2014, Magyar Telekom held talks with prospective buyers but decided against a private sale. The Lazar scandal had caused a public outcry, as critics accused the company of bending to political pressure. Executives wanted the deal to be beyond reproach, so an open bidding process was announced in June 2015 and overseen by Ernst and Young, an international accountancy firm.

The winner was named in November 2015: a firm called New Wave Media, which outbid two rival companies.

New Wave's profile immediately raised eyebrows. Their bid was financed by funds controlled by two banks, one owned by Mr. Orban's government, and another owned by Tamas Szemerey, a cousin of one of Mr. Orban's former ministers. In addition, New Wave was part-owned by Mr. Szemerey's longtime business partner, company records show.

Mr. Szemerey had made earlier attempts to buy Origo directly. But by his own telling, Magyar Telekom executives had discouraged such a direct attempt, on the grounds that he would be perceived as too close to the government.

Yet Mr. Szemerey ended up helping to pay for Origo all the same.

There was no evidence of favoritism: New Wave had simply made the highest bid. But bolstered by money from the state, New Wave could afford to pay whatever it took to avoid the outlet being sold to businesses not aligned with the government.

"We did not want it in the hands of Soros, or in the hands of people outside Hungary, or people who wanted to influence Hungarian politics against the Hungarian government," Mr. Szemerey said in an interview.

Magyar Telekom and Deutsche Telekom declined to comment on Mr. Szemerey's contacts with Telekom officials, but said the deal had been conducted transparently.

Though nominally still private, Origo now became a vessel for the government. Bought in part with government money, Origo now published news that echoed the government's stance — in particular on migration, Mr. Soros and the European Union, whose officials have frequently criticized Mr. Orban.

Before, Origo had struggled financially. Now it was flush with government advertising revenue, which more than tripled after the sale. In 2017, the son of Mr. Orban's former finance minister became New Wave's chief executive, and government advertising revenues kept rising, even as Origo's coverage became even more aggressively pro-Orban.

At the time, the 2015 sale of Origo could have been considered an outlier. Then, Origo became one of just 31 outlets owned by Mr. Orban's allies, according to research by Atlatszo, an investigative news website.

Today, there are more than 500.

CHAPTER 3

In the Arts, Sciences and More

Instances of censorship occur outside of wartime and authoritarian regimes as well. Books are banned from schools and libraries because their content is deemed inappropriate in some way. Art exhibits are removed due to protest from offended parties. Governments censor scientific information to avoid causing mass panic. Even legal proceedings can be censored in news coverage by way of gag orders in the effort to ensure fair trials. In cases such as these, the reasons to censor are nuanced and often widely debated.

Is There Censorship?

ESSAY | BY RACHEL DONADIO | DEC. 19, 2004

IN ACCEPTING A lifetime achievement award from the National Book Foundation at a black-tie gala in Manhattan last month, Judy Blume, the doyenne of young-adult fiction, delivered herself of the following admonition: "Your favorite teacher — the one who made literature come alive for you, the one who helped you find exactly the book you needed when you were curious, or hurting, the one who was there to listen to you when you felt alone — could become the next target."

A target, that is, of censorship. Blume's books, which address sexuality and religion with a frankness that has made many a grown-up squeamish, have been among the books most frequently banned from public school libraries over the years, and so the author certainly knows whereof she speaks. Yet there was something slightly alarmist in Blume's remarks. In somber, insistent tones, she spoke as if the authorities were lurking behind the doors of the Marriott Marquis ballroom ready to burst in at any moment and break up the party.

Blume's speech perfectly captured the mood in certain literary circles these days, where air once thick with now banned cigarette smoke instead hangs heavy with talk of the C-word. But the kind of censorship Blume has faced concerns individual libraries choosing not to lend her books, or placing restrictions on who can borrow them. It isn't about government harassment, even though that's what Blume seemed to be implying.

The definition of censorship has loosened so much that the word has become nearly devoid of meaning. Long gone are the days when the government banned racy books like D. H. Lawrence's "Lady Chatterley's Lover," Henry Miller's "Tropic of Cancer" or James Joyce's "Ulysses." When it comes to the written word, censorship debates are no longer about taste and decency — although those issues are much in the news concerning the visual arts, television and radio. Instead, the debate over books tends to center on geopolitics, national security and foreign policy.

Today, most defenders of the written word are focusing their energies on opposing certain sections of the USA Patriot Act, chief among them Section 215, which states that federal investigators can review library and bookstore records under certain circumstances in terrorism investigations. Larry Siems, the director of international programs at the PEN American Center, strikes an oft-heard chorus when he denounces "the growing use of government surveillance and government intrusion into your creative space." This, in turn, feeds a concern "that the government is able to see more deeply into our intellectual lives," Siems says.

Where there is smoke, there may very well be fire, but there may also be mirrors. It's often hard to draw the line between perception and practice, between how certain government regulations are viewed and how they're actually being enforced. The very mention of the Patriot

Act is enough to drive many publishers, writers, librarians, bookstore owners, readers and concerned citizens into a near-paranoid frenzy at the idea that the government is intruding into their personal business, although few can cite specific instances in which that is the case.

Indeed, the marketing department of any given publishing house probably has far more power over free expression in America than any government office; if it decides a smart book won't sell, the publisher may not sign it. Attitudes are rampant, but facts are harder to find. And ultimately, grandstanding and self-righteousness obscure the fact that some cases do approach government censorship.

Consider two recent lawsuits. This fall, a group of publishers and Shirin Ebadi, a lawyer and leading women's rights advocate in Iran who won the Nobel Peace Prize in 2003, filed two separate lawsuits against the Treasury Department's Office of Foreign Assets Control, or OFAC, which places serious restrictions on importing written work by authors in Iran, Sudan, Cuba and other countries under United States trade embargo. Under these regulations, buying the rights to unwritten books or making significant editorial changes to written works without a license is considered "providing a service," and therefore akin to trading with the enemy, something punishable with jail time and fines of up to $1 million. Publishers argue that this regulation violates the First Amendment.

OFAC devotes most of its resources to investigating terrorist financing and narcotics trafficking, and the regulations are largely intended for those aims. Some of the regulations at issue have been on the books for decades — the Trading With the Enemy Act dates to 1917 — and since the 80's amendments have been added to exempt "informational materials" from being subject to sanctions. But the current fuss dates back to this spring, when the Office of Foreign Assets Control issued a particularly stiff response to a query from the Institute of Electrical and Electronic Engineers, which wanted to publish papers by scientists from countries under embargo. The Treasury office ruled that the institute could edit a manuscript from a country under embargo, and engage in peer review, but that making any "substantive or artistic alterations or enhancements of the manuscript" would be illegal without a license. Likewise, no publisher could market a book and no literary agent could sign an author from an embargoed country without a license.

This sent the publishers through the roof. In September, Arcade, an independent publisher; the international writers' organization PEN; the Association of American University Presses; and a division of the Association of American Publishers filed suit against the foreign assets office. "I think that censorship is the biggest danger that could confront this country, aside from physical attack," Richard Seaver, the editor in chief of Arcade Publishing, said in a recent interview in his comfortably cluttered Manhattan office. "Censorship is never dead. It can always rear its ugly head. The danger is greater today than in the past 30 years."

A month later, Ebadi — the Iranian human rights lawyer (and Iran's first Nobelist), who under the rules can't sell her memoir to an American publisher — filed her own suit, along with the Strothman Agency of Boston, which can't officially represent her. Ebadi raised the censorship question in an Op-Ed article in The Times last month (which she could publish because newspapers are exempt from some of the regulations). "If even people like me — those who advocate peace and dialogue — are denied the right to publish their books in the United States with the assistance of Americans, then people will seriously question the view of the United States as a country that advocates democracy and freedom everywhere," she wrote. "What is the difference between the censorship in Iran and this censorship in the United States? Is it not better to encourage a dialogue between Iranians and the American public?"

Salman Rushdie, the president of the board of trustees of the PEN American Center and an old hand at such debates, wrote in a declaration as part of the suit: "Writers in Iran, Cuba and Sudan cannot publish freely in their own countries. It is a tragic and dangerous irony that Americans may not freely publish the works of those writers here, either." Publishers say several books have been suspended or canceled pending the ruling, including "City of Columns: Historic Architecture of Havana" by Alejo Carpentier (Smithsonian Institution Press), "The Encyclopedia of Cuban Music" (Temple University Press) and a paper by geologists at Shiraz University in Iran for an issue of the journal Mathematical Geology. "Even if there isn't a single case where they actually prosecuted, there's a famous chilling effect," says Leon Friedman, a lawyer for PEN and Arcade who helped bring the lawsuit. "Publishers just won't take a chance."

Molly Millerwise, a spokeswoman for the Treasury Department, declined to comment on the lawsuits. She says that over the years, no more than a dozen license applications have been submitted, most of them since last year, and none have been denied, although some are still pending. She says the department encourages publishers to approach them with queries.

So why don't the publishers simply apply for a license? Just ask any self-respecting publisher. "I'm not going to ask permission," Seaver says. "That's the Iranian way of doing things." He says Arcade is going full speed ahead with "Strange Times, My Dear: The PEN Anthology of Contemporary Iranian Literature," which is due out in April. He acknowledges that the lawsuit might help draw attention to the book. "I think libraries will be more attentive because they will have to be. Booksellers, too."

You can't help getting the sense that there is a certain amount of public relations going on here. Ebadi could conceivably have sold the rights to her memoirs in Britain, and the British publisher could have subsequently sold the American rights. But that wasn't the point. "American readers deserve to be hearing directly from someone like Ebadi," says Wendy Strothman, the literary agent and former publishing executive who is informally representing Ebadi. Strothman says Ebadi might well have been able to get a license "because of her stature as a Nobel laureate," but the lawsuit was "a matter of principle." It's also not entirely clear whether the Treasury Department would allow an American publisher to import such a work from Britain. "There are so many weighing factors," Millerwise says.

Ebadi hasn't yet written her memoir. In her statement to the court, which reads a little like a book proposal, Ebadi says her book would discuss "how I became a lawyer, a judge and a law professor despite the obvious and often official obstacles women in Iran have had to face."

There certainly does seem to be a market for Iranian women's memoirs. Both lawsuits cite the success of Azar Nafisi's best-selling "Reading Lolita in Tehran," about a group of women who met weekly in secret to read forbidden works of Western literature, and of "Persepolis," Marjane Satrapi's graphic novel about growing up during the Iranian revolution. Nafisi emigrated to Washington in 1997, and Satrapi now lives in France; neither could have published her book in Iran. For her part, Nafisi says she finds the Treasury Department regulations "mind-boggling," and has written a letter to the court supporting Ebadi's suit. "I understand sometimes there might be sanctions," Nafisi says. "The point about this law is the people it will hurt are the people who have been suppressed in that country anyway." She continues: "The principle of publishing should be understanding, should be more knowledge. On principle I think you have to publish even Ayatollah Khomeni!"

Although the Treasury rules have been on the books for ages, the lawsuits play into the literary world's general dislike of the Bush administration. When the regulations "reached international ears, it was a very clear example to the international community of a kind of American cultural closed-mindedness," Larry Siems of PEN says. "I spent a lot of time explaining to my international colleagues that this was not this administration's doing."

Both lawsuits may very well be settled in the coming months. In November the Treasury Department asked for a one-month extension so it could file its response to the suits in January. "The reason for the requested extension is that the parties anticipate that there may be developments with a possibly significant effect on the posture of the case, such that the briefing may need to be refocused or may even prove unnecessary," the Treasury Department's attorney wrote to the judge, according to a copy of the letter provided by the Strothman Agency's lawyer. The group of publishers received a similar letter, one of its lawyers said. Both sets of plaintiffs agreed to the extension. It remains to be seen whether the Treasury Department will adjust its regulations or rule only on those specific cases.

Meanwhile, these lawsuits have provided many in the literary and publishing world with a cause — one that's far more concrete than nebulous fears about the Bush administration or the Patriot Act. And it's certainly more satisfying to focus on censorship than on the future of publishing. It also seems to get the creative juices flowing. "There's always a clash, an underlying tension, between politics, which is basically trying to keep the status quo, and literature, which is constantly questioning the status quo," Nafisi says. "This tension between politics and culture is healthy. Each of us are playing our roles." You might say that all this conflict about infringements — both real and perceived — on free expression bodes well for free expression.

ESSAY EDITORS' NOTE: December 19, 2004, Sunday
An essay on Page 16 of the Book Review today, "Is There Censorship?," discusses government regulations on publishing the work of writers in Iran, Sudan, Cuba and possibly other countries under United States economic sanctions. The essay cites Treasury Department rulings that buying the rights to books not yet written, or making substantive alterations or enhancements in written works from those countries, might be illegal and punishable unless each transaction was licensed in advance by the department. On Wednesday, after the Book Review had gone to press, the Treasury issued a new general license permitting "all transactions necessary and ordinarily incident to the publishing and marketing of manuscripts, books, journals and newspapers" with people in those countries, provided the publishers do not deal with representatives of their governments.

Crying Censorship

OPINION | BY STANLEY FISH | AUG. 24, 2008

SALMAN RUSHDIE, self-appointed poster boy for the First Amendment, is at it again. This time he's not standing up for free expression on his own behalf, but on behalf of another author, Sherry Jones, whose debut novel about the prophet Muhammad's child bride had been withdrawn by Random House after consultants warned that its publication "could incite racial conflict."

Random House is also Rushdie's publisher, and his response to the news was to send an e-mail to The Associated Press. (I never thought of that; maybe I'll try it myself.) It read, "I am very disappointed to hear that my publishers, Random House, have canceled another author's novel because of their concerns about possible Islamic reprisals. This is censorship by fear and it sets a very bad precedent indeed."

This little brouhaha has been widely reported and commentators have tended to endow it with large philosophical and political implications (the Danish cartoon controversy of 2005 and the murder of Dutch filmmaker Theo van Gogh are often referenced). A story in The Times of London online edition describes it "the latest showdown between Islam and the Western tradition of free speech." One respondent declared bravely, "I will never buy another book published by Random House," and added, in a frenzy of patriotism, "We are Americans. We are free to choose what we want to read."

Well, I guess we are, although that wouldn't be my definition of what it means to be an American. It is also true, however, that Random House is free to publish or decline to publish whatever it likes, and its decision to do either has nothing whatsoever to do with the Western tradition of free speech or any other high-sounding abstraction.

Rushdie and the pious pundits think otherwise because they don't quite understand what censorship is. Or, rather, they conflate the colloquial sense of the word with the sense it has in philosophical and legal contexts. In the colloquial sense, censorship occurs whenever we don't say or write something because we fear adverse consequences, or because we feel that what we would like to say is inappropriate in the circumstances, or because we don't want to hurt someone's feelings. (This is often called self-censorship. I call it civilized behavior.)

From the other direction, many think it censorship when an employee is disciplined or not promoted because of something he or she has said, when people are ejected from a public event because they are judged to be disrupting the proceedings, or when a newspaper declines to accept an advertisement, rejects an op-ed or a letter, or fails to report on something others think important. But if censorship is the proper name for all these actions, then censorship is what is being practiced most of the time and is in fact the norm rather than the (always suspect) exception.

But censorship is not the proper name; a better one would be judgment. We go through life adjusting our behavior to the protocols and imperatives of different situations, and often the adjustments involve deciding to refrain from saying something. It's a calculation, a judgment call. It might be wise or unwise, prudent or overly cautious, but it has nothing to with freedom of expression.

Judgment is also what employers exercise when they determine that something an employee has said or written so undermines the enterprise that it warrants dismissal. To the objection that such an action would amount to a curtailing of the employee's First Amendment rights, the Supreme Court has answered (in Connick v. Myers, 1983) only if the speech in question were directed at a matter of public concern; otherwise, wrote Justice Byron White, "when close working relationships are essential to fulfilling ... responsibilities, a wide degree of deference to the employer's judgment is appropriate."

Many thought it was censorship in 2004 when ABC refused to air an ad critical of President Bush during the Super Bowl, or when affiliates of the same network refused to show "Saving Private Ryan" out of a fear that under new regulations they would be subject to fines for presenting material containing profanity and graphic violence. Again, these decisions may have been ill-advised or pusillanimous, but they were not blows against the First Amendment and they were not censorship. No doubt the ad played on some other day, and no one is interdicting the showing of the movie, which is readily available in any number of venues. Nor is it censorship when a library decides not to purchase a book or to withdraw a book from the shelves. You can still get it from Amazon.com. or buy it in Borders.

But if none of these actions fits the definition of censorship, what does?

It is censorship when Germany and other countries criminalize the professing or publication of Holocaust denial. (I am not saying whether this is a good or a bad idea.) It is censorship when in some countries those who criticize the government are prosecuted and jailed. It was censorship when the United States Congress passed the Sedition Act of 1798, stipulating that anyone who writes with the intent to bring the president or Congress or the government "into contempt or disrepute" shall be "punished by a fine not exceeding two thousand dollars and by imprisonment not exceeding two years." Key to these instances is the fact that (1) it is the government that is criminalizing expression and (2) that the restrictions are blanket ones. That is, they are not the time, manner, place restrictions that First Amendment doctrine traditionally allows; they apply across the board. You shall not speak or write about this, ever. That's censorship.

So what Random House did was not censorship. (Some other press is perfectly free to publish Jones's book, and one probably will.) It may have been cowardly or alarmist, or it may have been good business, or it may have been an attempt to avoid trouble that ended up buying trouble. But whatever it was, it doesn't rise to the level of constitutional or philosophical concern. And it is certainly not an episode in some "showdown between Islam and the Western tradition of free speech." Formulations like that at once inflate a minor business decision and trivialize something too important and complex to be reduced to a high-school civics lesson about the glories of the First Amendment.

STANLEY FISH is a professor of humanities and law at Florida International University, in Miami.

Bullying and Censorship

EDITORIAL | BY THE NEW YORK TIMES | DEC. 6, 2010

IN AN APPALLING ACT of political cowardice, the Smithsonian Institution last week removed "A Fire in My Belly," a four-minute video clip, from an exhibit called "Hide/Seek" at the National Portrait Gallery. The privately financed show explores identity, gender and homosexuality in American portraiture.

The video, by David Wojnarowicz, is a moving, anguished reflection on the artist's impending death from AIDS. It shows very quick glimpses of challenging and, at times, disturbing images, including masks, a meatpacking plant, various objects on fire and the artist undressing himself.

One of those images, 11 seconds of ants crawling on a crucifix, drew an outraged denunciation from the Catholic League, a lay civil rights organization that receives no church financing. It called the video "hate speech" and said it was designed to "assault the sensibilities of Christians." A spokesman for Representative John Boehner, the incoming House speaker, called for the Smithsonian to shut down the exhibition or "be prepared to face tough scrutiny" under the new Republican majority.

Secretary G. Wayne Clough of the Smithsonian immediately yielded, removing the video from the exhibit. His excuse was that the video "was detracting from the entirety of the exhibition." That is absurd. The exhibition is supposed to deal with culturally challenging images. Indeed, some of the most important roles of art and of museums are to challenge, disturb and enlighten.

The Catholic League is entitled to protest, as are members of Congress, although the bullying from Mr. Boehner's office was chilling. Mr. Clough had a responsibility to defend this work and to reject censorship. He failed. On Monday, the Smithsonian announced that the exhibit will remain open, as planned, until Feb. 13, but without Mr. Wojnarowicz's video. That is not remotely good enough.

'Censors At Work,' By Robert Darnton

REVIEW | BY ALBERTO MANGUEL | NOV. 7, 2014

THE IMPULSE TO CENSOR is as old as the impulse to create. Plato, not the most liberal of men, suggested that the work of storytellers should be carefully examined "and what they do well we must pass and what not, reject." His purpose was to moralize literature; others, over the centuries, have offered equally noble motives. Ibn Khaldun, the great Arab historian, reported that in the seventh century, when Muslim soldiers invaded Persia, they discovered an extraordinary number of books; wishing to carry them off as loot, they asked Omar bin al-Khattab, second caliph of the Muslims, for permission. Omar's answer became legendary and was applied to other book destructions: "Throw them in the river! If they hold a guide to the Truth, God has given us a better guide in the Holy Quran. And if they hold nothing but lies, may God rid us of them." In our own time, the president of Turkey, Recep Tayyip Erdogan, forced Google and Twitter to remove content objected to by his government or risk blackouts, arguing that "these regulations do not impose any censorship at all on the Internet.... On the contrary, they make it safer and freer." Morality, truth, civilized society, freedom: All these have been invoked to defend what most people would understand as censorship.

But what exactly is censorship? This is the question with which Robert Darnton, the foremost historian of the book and the art of reading, begins his enthralling new volume, "Censors at Work." "Rather than starting with a definition and then looking for examples that conform to it," Darnton writes, "I have proceeded by interrogating censors themselves." The censors Darnton has interrogated belong to three very different historical settings: the Old Regime in France, British rule in India and the Communist state that existed under the name of the German Democratic Republic from 1949 to 1990. Darnton spoke with the German censors in the flesh, and with the ghosts of the

French and British ones through the vast archives they left behind. Thankfully for Darnton, thankfully for his readers, the one incontrovertible fact about censors is that they love paperwork.

Most historians of censorship, like Fernando Báez in his excellent "A Universal History of the Destruction of Books," assume that the censor's task has always been to forbid and destroy. Darnton shows that this is not the case. The first period he explores is also that with which he is most familiar, having written numerous books on 18th-century France. He begins by looking at a book printed in Paris in 1722 that carries the "approbation and privilege of the king." These approbations, as Darnton notes, qualify as censorship because they were "delivered by royal censors."

But rather than what modern readers would expect from a censoring hand, they are something closer to our present-day blurbs. One of these censors, a professor at the Sorbonne, notes: "I had pleasure in reading it; it is full of fascinating things." Another, a theologian, remarks with obvious delight that a book inspired "that sweet but avid curiosity that makes us want to continue further." As Darnton makes clear, censorship under the Bourbon monarchy was not a system of limitations; it was a way of channeling the power of print through the figure of the king and his representatives, asserting royal authority over everything, even the word. Royal censors were not mainly on the outlook for subversive voices: instead, they worked like copy editors, concerned with matters of style, grammar, readability and originality of thought, even going so far as correcting spelling and redoing math. A book approved by the king should not be badly written.

In the 1750s, the term "bureaucracy" appeared in France to describe the increased reliance of the system on a complex hierarchy of clerks. Bureaucracy both simplified and complicated the job of the censor by requiring the participation of all kinds of other actors in the process of filtering and allotting or denying privileges to books. Darnton traces this system through a web that included not only authors, printers and booksellers, but also peddlers, smugglers and warehouse keepers. As

A 19th-century French engraving protests censorship; the censor with his scissors is on the left.

becomes evident, censorship was not a problem that concerned only the intellectuals.

During the second period explored by Darnton, that of British rule in India, Darnton says, "in principle, the press was free but the state imposed severe sanctions whenever it felt threatened." He relates the case of a certain James Long, an Anglo-Irish missionary in Bengal, who attempted "to survey everything printed in Bengali between April 1857 and April 1858" in order to help the newly established Indian Civil Service track what was being written. If censorship in 18th-century France manifested itself primarily as a sort of literary criticism, in British India the main impulse seems to have been an obsessive ethnographic curiosity. Long appears to have been driven by an interest in all aspects of the "other" culture — philology, folklore, religion and Hindu philosophy — rather than by any concern with seditious plotting against British rule.

But Long's interest in Bengali literature led to his downfall. In 1861, he arranged for the publication in English of a melodrama about the oppression of native workers by British planters that he thought might interest the public back home. The planters accused him of libel; Long was found guilty, fined a thousand rupees and sentenced to a month in prison. British law in India upheld freedom of speech, so the authorities needed to employ other means of controlling the spread of possibly subversive voices. The laws against libel and sedition became the British Empire's censorship tools in the subcontinent.

In investigating the 40-odd-year rule of Communists in East Germany, Darnton was able to meet censors in person: a man and a woman who worked for the state and had never before met an American. They disliked the word "censorship." What they did, they explained, was "planning," since in a socialist system literature was "planned" like everything else. Darnton shows how, behind their bureaucratic activities, lay a complicated tangle of motives — ideological ones certainly, but also tactical politics and personal revenge. So ingrained was the German censors' notion of duty to this system that even after the dissolution of the Communist state, they continued to report for work.

This last example of censorship is, of the three chosen by Darnton, the one that comes closest to the popular understanding of the term. On Nov. 25, 1988, the East German novelist Christoph Hein delivered a daring speech at a congress of the Authors Union in Berlin, urging the abolition of censorship. "The printing-authorization procedure," Hein said, "supervision by the state, or to put it briefly and no less clearly, the censorship of publishing houses and books, of publishers and authors, is outmoded, useless, paradoxical, hostile to humanity, hostile to the people, illegal and punishable." Hein's words are, in their essence, true at any time in the embattled history of censorship, even today. Considering electronic censorship in China and the unrestricted surveillance of the American National Security Agency, Darnton asks: "Has modern technology produced a new kind of power, which has led to an imbalance between the role of the state and the rights of its citizens?"

As Darnton clearly shows, the labors of censors affect not only books and their makers, but vast sections of society. There are two possible ways of looking at censorship, he says: a narrow one, concentrating exclusively on the censors' strategies, and another, more generous one that considers literature "as a cultural system embedded in a social order." It's obvious which of the two Darnton believes is the most important.

CENSORS AT WORK
How States Shaped Literature
By Robert Darnton
Illustrated. 316 pp. W. W. Norton & Company. $27.95.

ALBERTO MANGUEL's latest book, "Curiosity," will be published in the spring.

Australian Furor Over Chinese Influence Follows Book's Delay

BY JACQUELINE WILLIAMS | NOV. 20, 2017

SYDNEY, AUSTRALIA — The book was already being promoted as an explosive exposé of Chinese influence infiltrating the highest levels of Australian politics and media. But then, months before it was set to hit bookstore shelves, its publisher postponed the release, saying it was worried about lawsuits.

The decision this month to delay the book, "Silent Invasion: How China Is Turning Australia into a Puppet State," has set off a national uproar, highlighting the tensions between Australia's growing economic dependence on China and its fears of falling under the political control of the rising Asian superpower.

Critics have drawn parallels to decisions this year by high-profile academic publishers in Europe to withhold articles from readers in China that might anger the Communist Party.

But the case has struck a particularly sensitive nerve in Australia, where the book's delay is the latest in a series of incidents that have raised concerns about what many here see as the threat from China to freedom of expression.

"The decision by Allen & Unwin to stall publication of this book almost proves the point that there's an undue level of Chinese influence in Australia," said Prof. Rory Medcalf, head of the National Security College at Australian National University. Allen & Unwin is one of Australia's largest publishers.

In the yet-unpublished book, the author, Clive Hamilton, a well-known intellectual and professor at Charles Sturt University in Australia, describes what he calls an orchestrated campaign by Beijing to influence Australia and silence China's critics.

In one chapter, according to Mr. Hamilton, the book asserts that senior Australian journalists were taken on junkets to China in order to "shift their opinions" so they would present China in a more positive light.

In another chapter, he said the book details what he calls links between Australian scientists and researchers at Chinese military universities, which he said had led to a transfer of scientific know-how to the People's Liberation Army.

The book had been scheduled to be published in April, and Mr. Hamilton had already turned in a manuscript. But Allen & Unwin, based in Sydney, suddenly informed him on Nov. 2 that it wanted to postpone publishing because of legal concerns.

Mr. Hamilton responded by demanding the return of the publication rights, effectively canceling the book's publication by Allen & Unwin. Mr. Hamilton says he will seek another publisher.

Mr. Hamilton said the decision had been made for fear of angering Beijing, and shows China's ability to limit what information Australians can see — exactly the sort of influence that he said he warned about in his book.

"This is the first case, I believe, where a major Western publisher has decided to censor material critical of China in its home country," Mr. Hamilton said in an interview. "Many people are deeply offended by this attack on free speech, and people see a basic value that defines Australia being undermined."

In a statement, the publisher said it decided to hold off publishing the book, which would have been Mr. Hamilton's ninth with the company, until "certain matters currently before the courts have been decided."

It did not specify what those matters were.

"Clive was unwilling to delay publication and requested the return of his rights," the statement said.

However, Mr. Hamilton has disclosed an email that he said was sent to him on Nov. 8 by Allen & Unwin's chief executive, Robert Gorman. The email explained the decision to delay the book's release: "April 2018 was too soon to publish the book and allow us to adequately guard against potential threats to the book and the company from possible action by Beijing."

"Our lawyer pointed to recent legal attacks by Beijing's agents of influence against mainstream Australian media organizations," the email said.

The contents of the email have been widely reported by the local news media. When asked for comment, Allen & Unwin declined to confirm or deny its authenticity. Mr. Gorman has not gone public to deny the email's authenticity.

Mr. Hamilton said the publisher was probably referring to two defamation cases that are currently in the courts aimed at two Australian media companies: the Australian Broadcasting Corporation, a major television company, and Fairfax Media, a newspaper publisher.

One of the suits was filed by Chau Chak Wing, a Chinese-Australian businessman who has been a major donor in Australian politics. Dr. Chau is seeking damages from the Australian Broadcasting Corporation for a TV news report that the suit says damaged his personal and professional reputation.

That report, which was shown on a popular current affairs program, said the Australian Security Intelligence Organization, the domestic spy agency, had warned political parties against accepting contributions from two ethnic Chinese, of whom one was Dr. Chau, because of what the report called ties to the Chinese government.

Dr. Chau has long said his campaign contributions are entirely legal and unrelated to the Chinese government.

The news report prompted a heated debate in Australia over how vulnerable its democratic political system is to foreign influence, especially from China.

The question of Chinese interference is a delicate one for Australia, an American ally that has embraced Beijing as its largest trade partner and welcomed Chinese investors, immigrants and students in large numbers.

"The book shows in great detail the problem of Chinese influence in Australia is much deeper than we thought," said Mr. Hamilton, a prolific author who in 2009 received the Order of Australia, one of the country's highest honors, for "service to public debate and policy development." "I think some of the material I've uncovered have been a shock even to our intelligence agencies," he said.

James Leibold, a professor of politics and Asian studies at La Trobe University in Melbourne, Australia, said the decision to withhold such a book, especially one written by a noted author like Mr. Hamilton, underscored China's growing ability to pressure publishers and other media companies.

Last month, Springer Nature, one of the world's largest academic publishers, came under criticism for self-censorship after it bowed to Chinese government requests to block hundreds of articles on its Chinese website that touched on delicate topics like Taiwan, Tibet and Chinese politics.

In August, another publisher, Cambridge University Press, admitted to removing some 300 articles from the Chinese website of China Quarterly, an academic journal, that mentioned issues like the 1989 Tiananmen massacre.

Experts say Allen & Unwin, the Australian publisher, has gone a step further by delaying access to a book to readers outside of China.

"Australia is a bellwether," said Professor Medcalf of National Security College. "If dissent can be stifled here, then it can be stifled anywhere."

XIUZHONG XU contributed reporting from Melbourne, Australia.

Art Censorship at Guantánamo Bay

OPINION | BY ERIN THOMPSON | NOV. 27, 2017

MOATH AL-ALWI'S PRAYER RUG is stained with paint. Every day, he wakes before dawn and works for hours on an elaborate model ship made from scavenged materials — one of dozens of sculptures he has created since he was first detained at the Guantánamo Bay military prison in 2002. Mr. al-Alwi is considered a low value detainee, but is being held indefinitely. His art is his refuge.

The sails of Mr. al-Alwi's ships are made from scraps of old T-shirts. A bottle-cap wheel steers a rudder made with pieces of a shampoo bottle, turned with delicate cables of dental floss. The only tool Mr. al-Alwi uses to make these intricate vessels is a pair of tiny, snub-nosed scissors, the kind a preschooler might use. It is all he is allowed in his cell.

Three of Mr. al-Alwi's model ships are currently on view in an exhibit at John Jay College of Criminal Justice in New York City, along with 32 other paintings and sculptures from other prisoners or former detainees. My colleagues and I curated this exhibit after learning that many lawyers who have worked with detainees have file cabinets stuffed full of prisoners' art. In the atmosphere of surveillance and control that is Guantánamo, these artworks are among the only ways detainees have to communicate with the outside world.

But last week, the Miami Herald reported a change in military policy: The art of Mr. al-Alwi and the other remaining Guantánamo prisoners is now U.S. government property. The art will no longer leave prison confines and can now legally be destroyed. Attorneys for several prisoners were told the military intends to burn the art.

Art censorship and destruction are tactics fit for terrorist regimes, not for the U.S. military. The art poses no security threat: It is screened by experts who study the material for secret messages before it leaves the camp, and no art by current prisoners can be sold. Guantánamo detainees deserve basic human rights as they await trial. Taking away ownership of their art is both incredibly petty and utterly cruel.

Through this art, you can see what Guantánamo prisoners dream of in their cells, held for years without trial or without even having charges filed against them. They paint the things they wish they could see: sunsets, meadows, cityscapes and their homes. But most of all, they paint and sculpt the sea, rendering beaches, waves and boats in delicate colors and shapes. These prisoners have heard and smelled the sea for years, since the camp is only yards away from the Caribbean. But only for four days once, when a hurricane was approaching, did the guards take down the tarps that cover the fences, and allow prisoners to see it. The sea is central to their art, a symbol of freedom.

Making art is a profoundly human urge. Viewing this art has allowed thousands of visitors at John Jay College and elsewhere a chance to see that its makers are human beings. These detainees have been treated in fundamentally dehumanizing ways, from torture to denial of fair trials, and their art reminds us that we cannot ignore their condition.

Half of the artists featured in our exhibit, like hundreds of other detainees before them, were released after showing that they pose no threat to the United States. Burning Mr. al-Alwi's ships won't help the war on terror. Making art is the only form of therapy available at Guantánamo. Art helps detainees keep sane, meaning that those who are guilty will one day be fit to stand trial. And restricting and burning detainee art offers another excuse for terrorist groups to encourage their followers by pointing to an irrational exercise of absolute power.

For each of his model ships, Mr. al-Alwi ruffles cardboard into feathers to create an eagle-shaped prow. As he spends months creating each one, he imagines that he himself is an eagle, soaring over the sea. Unless the military reverses its cruel new policy, he can no longer even launch his fragile creations into the world, to be free in his place.

ERIN L. THOMPSON, an assistant professor at the John Jay College of Criminal Justice, is a co-curator of the exhibit "Ode to the Sea: Art from Guantánamo."

Seeing Terror Risk, U.S. Asks Journals to Cut Flu Study Facts

BY DENISE GRADY AND WILLIAM J. BROAD | DEC. 20, 2011

FOR THE FIRST TIME EVER, a government advisory board is asking scientific journals not to publish details of certain biomedical experiments, for fear that the information could be used by terrorists to create deadly viruses and touch off epidemics.

In the experiments, conducted in the United States and the Netherlands, scientists created a highly transmissible form of a deadly flu virus that does not normally spread from person to person. It was an ominous step, because easy transmission can lead the virus to spread all over the world. The work was done in ferrets, which are considered a good model for predicting what flu viruses will do in people.

The virus, A(H5N1), causes bird flu, which rarely infects people but has an extraordinarily high death rate when it does. Since the virus was first detected in 1997, about 600 people have contracted it, and more than half have died. Nearly all have caught it from birds, and most cases have been in Asia. Scientists have watched the virus, worrying that if it developed the ability to spread easily from person to person, it could create one of the deadliest pandemics ever.

A government advisory panel, the National Science Advisory Board for Biosecurity, overseen by the National Institutes of Health, has asked two journals, Science and Nature, to keep certain details out of reports that they intend to publish on the research. The panel said conclusions should be published, but not "experimental details and mutation data that would enable replication of the experiments."

The panel cannot force the journals to censor their articles, but the editor of Science, Bruce Alberts, said the journal was taking the recommendations seriously and would probably withhold some information — but only if the government creates a system to provide the missing information to legitimate scientists worldwide who need it.

The journals, the panel, researchers and government officials have been grappling with the findings for several months. The Dutch researchers presented their work at a virology conference in Malta in September.

Scientists and journal editors are generally adamant about protecting the free flow of ideas and information, and ready to fight anything that hints at censorship.

"I wouldn't call this censorship," Dr. Alberts said. "This is trying to avoid inappropriate censorship. It's the scientific community trying to step out front and be responsible."

He said there was legitimate cause for the concern about the researchers' techniques falling into the wrong hands.

"This finding shows it's much easier to evolve this virus to an extremely dangerous state where it can be transmitted in aerosols than anybody had recognized," he said. Transmission by aerosols means the virus can be spread through the air via coughing or sneezing.

Ever since the tightening of security after the terrorist attacks on Sept. 11, 2001, scientists have worried that a scientific development would pit the need for safety against the need to share information. Now, it seems, that day has come.

"It's a precedent-setting moment, and we need to be careful about the precedent we set," Dr. Alberts said.

Both studies of the virus — one at the Erasmus Medical Center in Rotterdam, in the Netherlands, and the other at the University of Wisconsin-Madison — were paid for by the National Institutes of Health. The idea behind the research was to try to find out what genetic changes might make the virus easier to transmit. That way, scientists would know how to identify changes in the naturally occurring virus that might be warning signals that it was developing pandemic potential. It was also hoped that the research might lead to better treatments.

Dr. Anthony Fauci, head of the National Institute of Allergy and Infectious Diseases, said the research addressed important public health questions, but added, "I'm sure there will be some people who say these experiments never should have been done."

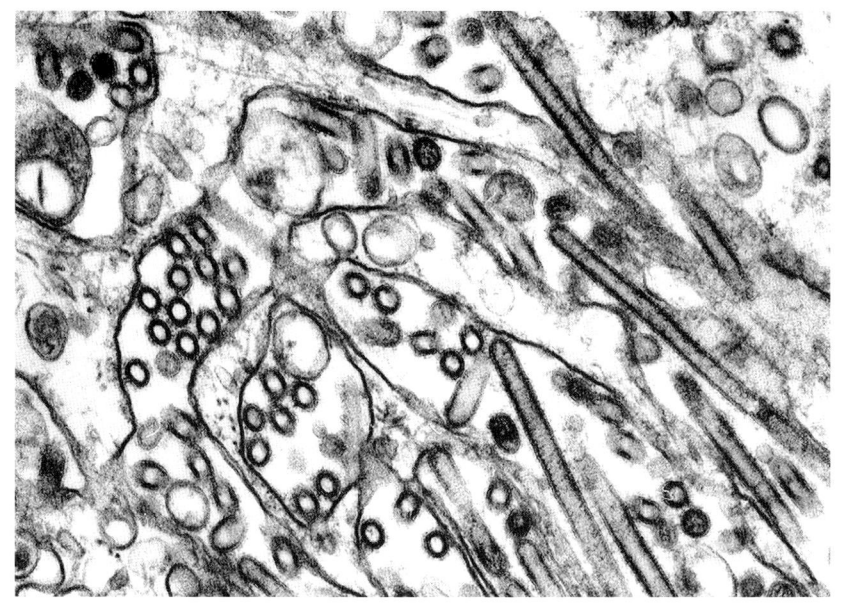

MEDIA FOR MEDICAL/UNIVERSAL IMAGES GROUP/GETTY IMAGES

The A(H5N1) virus, seen in dark gray, grown in MDCK cells, seen in light gray. The virus largely affects birds and rarely infects people, but it is highly deadly when it does.

Dr. Fauci said staff members at the institutes followed the results of the research and flagged it as something that the biosecurity panel should evaluate.

The lead researcher at the Erasmus center, Ron Fouchier, did not respond to requests for an interview. The center issued a statement saying that researchers there had reservations about the panel's recommendation, but would observe it.

The Wisconsin researcher, Yoshihiro Kawaoka, was out of the country and "not responding to queries," according to a spokesman for the university. But the school said its researchers would "respect" the panel's recommendations.

David R. Franz, a biologist who formerly headed the Army defensive biological lab at Fort Detrick, Md., is on the board and said its decision to intervene, made in the fall, was quite reasonable.

"My concern is that we don't give amateurs — or terrorists — information that might let them do something that could really cause a lot a harm," he said in an interview.

"It's a wake-up call," Dr. Franz added. "We need to make sure that our best and most responsible scientists have the information they need to prepare us for whatever we might face."

Amy Patterson, director of the office of biotechnology activities at the National Institutes of Health, in Bethesda, Md., said the recommendations were a first.

"The board in the past has reviewed manuscripts but never before concluded that communications should be restricted in any way," she said in a telephone interview. "These two bodies of work stress the importance of public health preparedness to monitor this virus."

Ronald M. Atlas, a microbiologist at the University of Louisville and past president of the American Society for Microbiology, who has advised the federal government on issues of germ terrorism, said the hard part of the recommendations would be creating a way to move forward in the research with a restricted set of responsible scientists.

He said that if researchers had a better understanding of how the virus works, they could develop better ways to treat and prevent illness. "That's why the research is done," he said.

The government, Dr. Atlas added, "is going to struggle with how to get the information out to the right people and still have a barrier" to wide sharing and inadvertently aiding a terrorist. "That's going to be hard."

Given that some of the information has already been presented openly at scientific meetings, and that articles about it have been sent out to other researchers for review, experts acknowledged that it may not be possible to keep a lid on the potentially dangerous details.

"But I think there will be a culture of responsibility here," Dr. Fauci said. "At least I hope there will."

The establishment of the board grew out of widespread fears stemming from the 2001 terrorist attacks on the United States and the ensuing strikes with deadly anthrax germs that killed or sickened 22 Americans.

The Bush administration called for wide controls on biological information that could potentially help terrorists. And the scientific community firmly resisted, arguing that the best defenses came with the open flow of information.

In 2002, Dr. Atlas, then the president-elect of the American Society for Microbiology, objected publicly to "anything that smacked of censorship."

The federal board was established in 2004 as a compromise and is strictly advisory. It has 25 voting members appointed by the secretary of health and human services, and has 18 ex officio members from other federal agencies.

Federal officials said Tuesday that the board has discussed information controls on only three or four occasions. The first centered on the genetic sequencing of the H1N1 virus that caused the 1918 flu pandemic, in which up to 100 million people died, making it one of the deadliest natural disasters in human history.

"We chose to recommend publication without any modifications," Dr. Franz, the former head of the Army lab, recalled. "The more our good scientists know about problems, the better prepared they are to fix them."

This fall, federal officials said, the board wrestled with the content of H5N1 papers to Science and Nature, and in late November contacted the journals about its recommendation to restrict information on the methods that the scientists used to modify the deadly virus.

"The ability of this virus to cross species lines in this manner has not previously been appreciated," said Dr. Patterson of the National Institutes of Health. "Everyone involved in this matter wants to do the proper thing."

Science and Censorship: A Duel Lasting Centuries

BY WILLIAM J. BROAD | DEC. 26, 2011

> We have consultations, which of the inventions and experiences which we have discovered shall be published, and which not; and take all an oath of secrecy for the concealing of those which we think fit to keep secret; though some of those we do reveal sometime to the State, and some not.
>
> Sir Francis Bacon, "New Atlantis"

THE SPECTER OF CENSORSHIP loomed over science last week with news that a federal advisory panel had asked two leading journals to withhold details of experiments out of fear that terrorists could use the information to make deadly flu viruses — the first time the government had interceded this way in biomedical research.

But science and secrecy go back centuries, their conflicting agendas often rooted in issues of war and advanced weaponry. Self-censorship — the kind of confidentiality being requested of the two journals, Science and Nature — was even mentioned by Bacon, the 17th-century British philosopher long credited with illuminating the scientific method.

Governments have repeatedly tried to keep scientific information secret in fields as diverse as math and cryptography, physics and nuclear science, optics and biology. Now the call for concealment is falling on one of the hottest of contemporary fields — virology, where researchers are tinkering with the fundamentals of life to better understand whether altered flu germs might set off deadly epidemics.

"It's a story with mythological resonance," said Steven Aftergood, director of the project on government secrecy at the Federation of American Scientists and the publisher of Secrecy News, an e-mail newsletter. "It reflects the view that knowledge is power and some kinds of knowledge have destructive power."

A lesson of history, Mr. Aftergood added, is that censorship often fails because science by nature is inherently open and gossipy — all the more so today because of instant communication and international travel.

"The notion that the boundaries of knowledge are defined by what is published by Science and Nature is quaint," he said, referring to the journals. "For better or worse, the way that knowledge is disseminated today is ever less dependent on the flagship journals. It's done by global scientific collaboration, draft papers, online publication, informal distribution of preprints, and on and on."

Last week, one of the flu scientists under pressure to limit publication raised a different objection. The journals are considering distributing the sensitive data to only a subset of responsible public health researchers, who could then use it to bolster germ defenses, but the scientist, Ron A. M. Fouchier, questioned how feasible that was.

The list of potential recipients "adds up to well over 100 organizations around the globe, and probably 1,000 experts," said Dr. Fouchier, of the Erasmus Medical Center in Rotterdam, the Netherlands. "As soon as you share information with more than 10 people, the information will be on the street."

Federal officials and private experts argued that governments have a duty to safeguard the public welfare — even if that means sometimes putting limits on scientific freedoms.

"I want science to be as open and transparent as possible," said David R. Franz, a biologist who formerly headed the Army defensive biological lab at Fort Detrick, Md. "My concern is that we don't give amateurs — or terrorists — information that might let them do something that could really cause a lot of harm."

And Bruce Alberts, the editor of Science, said the question for his journal was one not of federal intrusion but of "trying to avoid inappropriate censorship."

"It's the scientific community trying to step out front and be responsible," he said.

The most famous case of scientific suppression remains that of Galileo, who in 1633 was forced by the Roman Catholic Church to disavow his finding that the Earth revolves around the Sun. But over the centuries, the big clashes between science and the authorities came to center on highly destructive arms.

Starting in 1943, work in the United States on atom and hydrogen bombs led to a sprawling system of classification that in time involved millions of people and billions of dollars in security precautions. It was a world of safes and barbed wire, where individuals voluntarily gave up their rights of free speech.

In 1953, Julius and Ethel Rosenberg were executed after being convicted of passing bomb secrets to Moscow.

But atomic lore kept leaking. Today, nine nations have nuclear weapons, and dozens more are said to possess the secretive information, the technical skills and — in some cases — the materials needed to make them.

A new field came under scrutiny in the mid-1970s, when Washington tried to clamp down on publications in cryptography — the creating and breaking of coded messages. A breakthrough threatened to make it easer for the public to encrypt messages and harder for federal intelligence agencies to decipher them.

Agents of the National Security Agency — an organization so secret its initials were jokingly said to mean No Such Agency — paid a visit to Martin Hellman, an electrical engineer at Stanford University.

"They said, 'If you continue talking about this, you're going to cause grave harm to national security,' " he recalled.

Eventually, the government gave up, and the cryptography advances grew into a thriving global industry.

A new case arose in 1982 as the Reagan administration, eager to foil spies during the final days of the cold war, blocked the presentation of about 100 unclassified scientific papers at an international symposium on optical engineering. Protests erupted, and the administration soon backed down.

The terrorist attacks of Sept. 11, 2001 — and the ensuing strikes with deadly anthrax germs that killed or sickened 22 Americans — produced a wave of new jitters and restrictions. The main target was biology and its ability to make deadly micro-organisms.

The Bush administration pulled thousands of sensitive patents, papers and documents from public access, and debate erupted over whether journals and scientists at the frontiers of biology should accept federal restrictions. Many argued that the benefits of open inquiry — including new ways to fight terrorists — outweighed the theoretical costs.

"Terrorism feeds on fear, and fear feeds on ignorance," said Abigail A. Salyers, president of the American Society of Microbiology.

But in 2003, the editors of Science, Nature and The Proceedings of the National Academy of Sciences issued a joint declaration saying that occasions might indeed arise when a paper "should be modified, or not be published."

That day now seems to have arrived for advanced biology, at least in terms of developing a plan of response to the federal request. Publication of the two scientific reports — from the University of Wisconsin-Madison and the Erasmus Medical Center in the Netherlands — has been paused until the journal editors decide how to proceed.

Dr. Alberts, the editor of Science, laid considerable responsibility at the feet of the federal government.

"Our response," he said in a statement issued last week, "will be heavily dependent upon the further steps taken by the U.S. government to set forth a written, transparent plan to ensure that any information that is omitted from the publication will be provided to all those responsible scientists who request it, as part of their legitimate efforts to improve public health and safety."

Asked if he saw the federal panel as overreacting, Mr. Aftergood of the Federation of American Scientists said no.

"They're posing a question," he replied, "not issuing orders."

"There's a world of difference between the government imposing the heavy hand of censorship and this board saying to take a second look," Mr. Aftergood added. "I think they're doing what they should do, which is to call attention to a difficult case. It's the journals that will have to make the final decision."

Don't Censor Influenza Research

OPINION | BY HOWARD MARKEL | FEB. 1, 2012

ANN ARBOR, MICH. — In December, the National Science Advisory Board for Biosecurity made an unprecedented request: it asked the editors of the journals Nature and Science not to publish certain details in two papers describing experiments in which scientists created a highly transmissible form of the deadly H5N1 influenza virus in ferrets. The board's primary concern was that terrorists might use the data to weaponize influenza.

In the weeks since, supporters of the board's decision have issued warnings against publishing these papers in their entirety — and some have even called for destroying the new form of the virus. To calm matters, the scientific teams conducting the work agreed to a 60-day moratorium on their research. Starting Feb. 16, the World Health Organization will hold an international meeting to discuss how best to proceed.

Such caution, though well intentioned, is misplaced. The censorship of influenza research will do little to prevent its misuse by evildoers — and it may well hinder our ability to stop influenza outbreaks, whether natural or otherwise, when they do occur.

In this case, censorship is too little, too late. The data generated by one of the research teams was already presented at a conference in Malta in September, where copies of the paper were distributed. But even if the data weren't already available, the key details could likely be inferred from other information that is already available. I recently spoke with several prominent influenza scientists, all of whom agreed that, based on the knowledge that certain mutations can make H5N1 highly transmissible in ferrets, they could consult previously published literature and probably figure out what those mutations are.

A terrorist-generated pandemic is a worrisome threat, but there are reasons not to be overly preoccupied with the prospect. Even if terrorists got their hands on the new data, it's not certain they could weaponize the virus: no one knows for certain that the virus's transmissibility and virulence in ferrets means transmissibility and virulence in humans. In any event, the influenza virus, highly variable in its power and spread, is not an optimal terrorist weapon, not least because no one would know for sure if it was unleashed by a terrorist or natural forces.

A naturally occurring influenza pandemic is a far graver threat. And censorship of influenza research makes it harder to predict, treat and prevent such pandemics. Although modern medicine has made major advances since the deadly 1918 flu pandemic, we still know woefully little about the virus's complex biology. Before the current controversy, the National Science Advisory Board for Biosecurity, which President George W. Bush created in 2004, reviewed two papers on the genetic sequencing of the 1918 influenza virus; those papers were published in 2005 without redactions — or negative consequences. As a result, we now know the valuable fact that the changes in the 1918 H1N1 virus that made it so effective at infecting humans were *not* found in the 2009 H1N1 pandemic virus (sometimes called swine flu).

In the years since the 9/11 attacks, we've witnessed a disturbing trend in the oversight of sensitive science. The threat of terrorism prompted the Bush administration to create, in 2002, a broad and hazy designation for information called "sensitive but unclassified," or S.B.U. Unlike classified material, which can be viewed by select scientists and officials with proper security clearance or on a need-to-know basis, a body of work designated as S.B.U. can become virtually inaccessible to anyone.

According to a 2007 report by the National Academy of Sciences, S.B.U. designations proliferated not only among agencies within the security architecture, like the Defense Department, but also those far from it, like the Department of Health and Human Services. Several prominent scientists, including Donald Kennedy, the former editor of Science, have publicly worried that the federal government is thwarting scientific advancement.

This is the atmosphere in which the National Science Advisory Board for Biosecurity is operating. Until this most recent controversy, the board had reviewed only a few papers, requesting no redactions. It is not clear how the board proposes that the government categorize data that the board deems censorable. Will it recommend that specific studies be labeled S.B.U.? Or will it recommend traditionally classifying such data? And how might such recommendations inhibit future scientific research that looks to build on such discoveries?

Until these questions are better answered, we have reason to be concerned about any recommendations the federal government makes to censor science.

HOWARD MARKEL, a professor of the history of medicine at the University of Michigan, is the author of "When Germs Travel: Six Major Epidemics That Have Invaded America Since 1900 and the Fears They Have Unleashed."

Anti-Vaccine Activists Have Taken Vaccine Science Hostage

OPINION | BY MELINDA WENNER MOYER | AUG. 4, 2018

AMERICANS WHO DON'T want to vaccinate are increasingly getting their way: A June study found that, over the past decade, the number of philosophical vaccine exemptions rose in two-thirds of the states that allow them.

What drives these wrongheaded decisions is fear — fear that vaccines are somehow dangerous, even though research shows the opposite. And these choices have consequences. The 2015 Disneyland measles outbreak sickened at least 125 people, many of them unvaccinated.

As a science journalist, I've written several articles to quell vaccine angst and encourage immunization. But lately, I've noticed that the cloud of fear surrounding vaccines is having another nefarious effect: It is eroding the integrity of vaccine science.

In February I was awarded a fellowship by the nonpartisan Alicia Patterson Foundation to report on vaccines. Soon after, I found myself hitting a wall. When I tried to report on unexpected or controversial aspects of vaccine efficacy or safety, scientists often didn't want to talk with me. When I did get them on the phone, a worrying theme emerged: Scientists are so terrified of the public's vaccine hesitancy that they are censoring themselves, playing down undesirable findings and perhaps even avoiding undertaking studies that could show unwanted effects. Those who break these unwritten rules are criticized.

The goal is to protect the public — to ensure that more people embrace vaccines — but in the long-term, the approach will backfire. Our arsenal of vaccines is exceptional, but it could always be better. Progress requires scientific candor and a willingness to ask inconvenient questions.

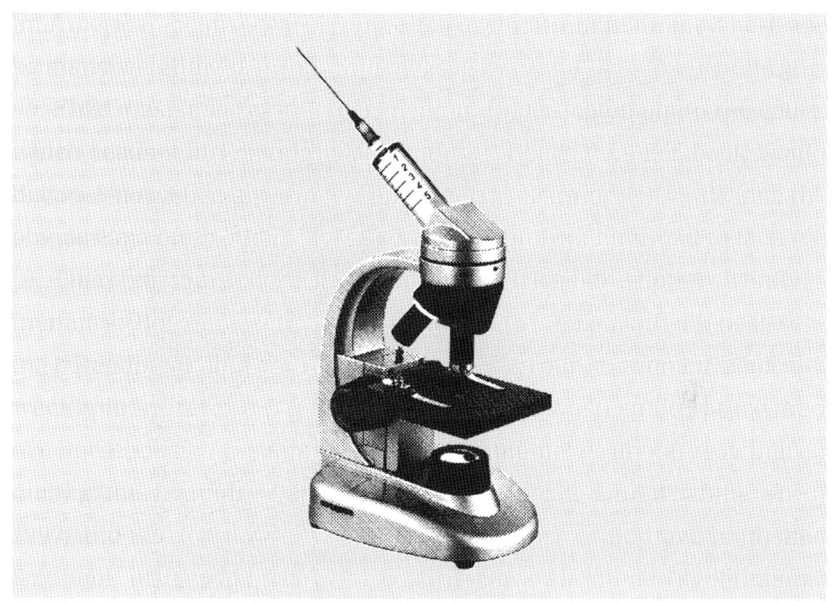

OLIVER MUNDAY

Here's a case that typifies this problem and illustrates how beneficial it can be when critical findings get published. In 2005, Lone Simonsen, who was then with the National Institute of Allergy and Infectious Diseases, and her colleagues published a study in JAMA Internal Medicine showing that the flu vaccine prevented fewer deaths than expected in people over 65.

"I had interesting conversations with vaccine people. They said, 'What are you doing, Lone? You are ruining everything,' " recalls Dr. Simonsen, who is now a global public health researcher at George Washington University. Her work helped lead to the development of a more effective flu vaccine for older people, yet she felt ostracized. "I felt it personally, because I wasn't really invited to meetings," she says. "It took a good decade before it was no longer controversial."

It's understandable for scientists to be nervous. The internet has made it easy for anti-vaccine activists to mislead. Dr. Simonsen's study, for instance, inspired a story with the ridiculous headline "Flu Vaccines Are Killing Senior Citizens, Study Warns."

But concerns over what these groups might do are starting to take precedence over scientific progress.

"Scientists' perception of public irrationality is having an impact on our ability to rationally discuss things that deserve discussion," says Andrew Read, the director of the Center for Infectious Disease Dynamics at Pennsylvania State University. Dr. Read studies how pathogens evolve in response to vaccines, and he is fiercely pro-vaccine — his goal is to keep the shots effective. He says he has had unpleasant encounters at scientific conferences; colleagues have warned him, for instance, not to talk too openly about his work. "I have felt the pressure — and for that matter the responsibility — acutely," he says.

In 2009, Danuta Skowronski, the lead epidemiologist in the division of Influenza and Emerging Respiratory Pathogens at the British Columbia Center for Disease Control, and her colleagues stumbled across unexpected data that suggested a link between seasonal flu shots and an increased risk for pandemic flu. The findings could not prove a causal link — perhaps people who get seasonal flu shots differ from those who don't in ways that make them more susceptible to pandemic strains. But one possible interpretation is that seasonal flu shots inhibit immunity to those strains. Dr. Skowronski's team replicated the findings in five different studies and then shared the data with trusted colleagues. "There was tremendous pushback," Dr. Skowronski recalls, and some questioned whether "the findings were appropriate for publication."

"I believed I had no right to not publish those findings," Dr. Skowronski says. "They were too important." The findings were submitted to three journals and underwent at least eight lengthy reviews before the final study was published in PloS Medicine.

Last September, researchers with the Vaccine Safety Datalink, a collaborative project between the Centers for Disease Control and Prevention and various health care organizations, published a study in the journal Vaccine that found an association — not a causal link, the authors were careful to note — between a flu vaccine and miscarriage.

Soon after, Paul Offit, the director of the Vaccine Education Center at the Children's Hospital of Philadelphia and co-inventor of a lifesaving rotavirus vaccine, said in The Daily Beast that the paper shouldn't have been published, in part because the study was small and conflicted with earlier research. He also suggested that the authors had cherry-picked their data — a charge they vehemently deny. One physician questioned in the popular blog Science-Based Medicine why the research had been funded in the first place.

Dr. Offit says that researchers should handle findings differently when there's a chance they might frighten the public. He thinks that small, inconclusive, worrying studies should not be published because they could do more harm than good. "Knowing that you're going to scare people, I think you have to have far more data," he explains.

But even an inconclusive paper can be important, others say, as it can spur the larger, more definitive studies that are needed. It should be "put out there for the scientific community, to look at it, see it, know about it, refine study design and go and look again," says Gregory Poland, a Mayo Clinic vaccinologist and the editor in chief of Vaccine. It is crucial, though, for researchers to carefully explain such results in their papers to prevent misinterpretation.

If a study scares parents away from vaccines, people could die. That's a big risk to take to protect the sanctity of scientific discourse. I was warned several times that covering this issue could leave me with "blood on my hands," too. But in the long run, isn't stifling scientific inquiry even more dangerous?

"If we get to the point where we don't want to look anymore because we don't want to know the answer, then we're in trouble," says Dr. Edward Belongia, one of the authors of the Vaccine study and director of the Center for Clinical Epidemiology and Population Health at the Marshfield Clinic Research Institute.

This is not to say that anyone is covering up major safety problems, by the way; critical studies generally concern minor issues in specific contexts. But scientists could one day miss more important problems if they embrace a culture that suppresses research. And at the end of the day, by cherry-picking data, public health researchers are doing "exactly what the anti-vaccine people do," Michael Osterholm, the director of the Center for Infectious Disease Research and Policy at the University of Minnesota, warns.

There's no question that bad vaccine science does not deserve a forum — and much of the research cited by anti-vaccine activists is very bad indeed. But good science needs to be heard even if some people will twist its meaning. One thing vaccine scientists and vaccine-wary parents have in common is a desire for the safest and most effective vaccines possible — but vaccines can't be refined if researchers ignore inconvenient data. Moreover, vaccine scientists will earn a lot more public trust, and overcome a lot more unfounded fear, if they choose transparency over censorship.

MELINDA WENNER MOYER is a science and health writer and a contributing editor at Scientific American.

Conservatives Fail the N.F.L.'s Free Speech Test

OPINION | BY DAVID FRENCH | MAY 24, 2018

THE UNITED STATES is in the grips of a free-speech paradox. At the same time that the law provides more protection to personal expression than at any time in the nation's history, large numbers of Americans feel less free to speak. The culprit isn't government censorship but instead corporate, community and peer intimidation.

Conservatives can recite the names of the publicly shamed from memory. There was Brendan Eich, hounded out of Mozilla for donating to a California ballot initiative that defined marriage as the union of a man and woman. There was James Damore, abruptly terminated from Google after he wrote an essay attributing the company's difficulty in attracting female software engineers more to biology and free choice than to systemic discrimination. On campus, the list is as long and grows longer every semester.

It is right to decry this culture of intolerance and advocate for civility and engagement instead of boycotts and reprisals. The cure for bad speech is better speech — not censorship. Take that message to the heartland, and conservatives cheer.

Until, that is, Colin Kaepernick chose to kneel. Until, that is, the president demanded that the N.F.L. fire the other players who picked up on his protest after he was essentially banished from the league.

That was when the conservative mob called for heads to roll. Conform or face the consequences.

On Wednesday, the mob won. The N.F.L. announced its anthem rules for 2018, and the message was clear: Respect the flag by standing for the national anthem or stay in the locker room. If you break the rules and kneel, your team can be fined for your behavior.

This isn't a "middle ground," as the N.F.L. claims. It's not a compromise. It's corporate censorship backed up with a promise of corporate punishment. It's every bit as oppressive as the campus or corporate attacks on expression that conservatives rightly decry.

But this is different, they say. This isn't about politics. It's about the *flag*.

I agree. It is different. Because it's about the flag, the censorship is even worse.

One of the most compelling expressions of America's constitutional values is contained in Justice Robert Jackson's 1943 majority opinion in West Virginia State Board of Education v. Barnette. At the height of World War II, two sisters, both Jehovah's Witnesses, challenged the state's mandate that they salute the flag in school. America was locked in a struggle for its very existence. The outcome was in doubt. National unity was essential.

But even in the darkest days of war, the court wrote liberating words that echo in legal history: "If there is any fixed star in our constitutional constellation, it is that no official, high or petty, can prescribe what shall be orthodox in politics, nationalism, religion, or other matters of opinion or force citizens to confess by word or act their faith therein."

Make no mistake, I want football players to stand for the anthem. I want them to respect the flag. As a veteran of the war in Iraq, I've saluted that flag in foreign lands and deployed with it proudly on my uniform. But as much as I love the flag, I love liberty even more.

The N.F.L. isn't the government. It has the ability to craft the speech rules its owners want. So does Google. So does Mozilla. So does Yale. American citizens can shame whomever they want to shame.

But what should they do? Should they use their liberty to punish dissent? Or should a free people protect a culture of freedom?

In our polarized times, I've adopted a simple standard, a civil liberties corollary to the golden rule: Fight for the rights of others that you would like to exercise yourself. Do you want corporations obliterating speech the state can't touch? Do you want the price of participation in public debate to include the fear of lost livelihoods? Then, by all means, support the N.F.L. Cheer Silicon Valley's terminations. Join the boycotts and shame campaigns. Watch this country's culture of liberty wither in front of your eyes.

The vice president tweeted news of the N.F.L.'s new policy and called it "#Winning." He's dead wrong. It diminishes the marketplace of ideas. It mocks the convictions of his fellow citizens. And it divides in the name of a false, coerced uniformity. Writing in the Barnette decision, Justice Jackson wisely observed, "As governmental pressure toward unity becomes greater, so strife becomes more bitter as to whose unity it shall be."

The N.F.L. should let players kneel. If it lets them kneel, it increases immeasurably the chances that when they do rise, they will rise with respect and joy, not fear and resentment. That's the "winning" America needs.

DAVID FRENCH is a senior writer at National Review.

Australian Gag Order Stokes Global Debate on Secrecy

ANALYSIS | BY DAMIEN CAVE | DEC. 14, 2018

SYDNEY, AUSTRALIA — There is a criminal case unfolding in Australia that shall not be named. The defendant is a figure with a global reputation, someone of great influence in the country and the world. The charges are serious and of significant public interest.

But publishing news about this case is illegal.

Judges in Australia and some other countries, including Britain, often issue gag orders that temporarily restrict the publication of information related to a criminal proceeding on the grounds that it might sway jurors or potential jurors.

Sometimes, judges even require the existence of these orders to be kept secret.

In this case, something unusual is happening — the sweep of the restrictions is so all-encompassing that the conflict between the public's right to know and the defendant's right to a fair trial is rippling across the internet and the world, touching news outlets and institutions in distant countries.

If you're not in Australia, you may have already read recent coverage of the case.

If you are in Australia or depend on online news from international organizations like The New York Times, The Associated Press or Reuters, you probably know nothing about it.

Gag orders, also known as suppression orders, are supposed to work that way. They usually apply to speech within a specific jurisdiction.

But the global nature of the internet has blurred the lines, giving local judges the power to threaten any website accessible to local residents, regardless of where the site or its journalists are based.

That includes The Times: The Times is not publishing the latest news of the case online, and it blocked delivery of the Friday print edition to Australia, to comply with the judge's order. The Times's lawyers in Australia have advised the organization that it is subject to local law because it maintains a bureau in the country.

Two Times journalists who have been covering the case would be at risk. The judge in the case has threatened journalists with contempt of court charges, which can bring up to five years in prison.

Some publications that have published the news have no full-time staff in Australia and face no such risk. Even naming them appears to be illegal.

But the battle reaches beyond one particular case. It's a contest of competing democratic values.

The core debate is an old one, pitting the right of the accused to a fair trial against the right of free speech, and of the public to know what's going on in the courtroom. Those poles are not mutually exclusive: Trials in Australia, as in the United States, are usually both open and fair.

"What you need for a fair trial are fair and unbiased jurors, not people who have been kept in the dark," said Kurt Wimmer, a media and technology lawyer who is a partner with Covington and Burling in Washington.

Because of the way technology has shifted the media landscape, gag orders now raise additional questions of scale and geography. The question now is whether a local judge, in protecting the right to a fair trial, should have the unilateral authority to silence journalists and publishers around the globe.

In the case at hand, a criminal matter involving someone whose previous position of power touched the lives of millions all over the world, the stakes are especially high. The defendant is well known, having played a public role with issues and institutions that inspire strong emotions, making bias harder to stamp out.

On the other side are not just journalists, but also those who were affected by the defendants' actions over many years in many places.

They demand accountability, and also claim a right to know, seeing secrecy as an accomplice to the crimes of the case.

A few news outlets without personnel or a corporate presence in Australia — and therefore no legal obligation or vulnerability — have already reported the case's latest developments online. On Twitter and Facebook, where the news can be found but is not ubiquitous, there has been praise from some Australians that the news was posted, and criticism from others worried that publication has jeopardized justice.

Other attempts to maneuver within the law have varied. One news site published the news online but tried to block access to the article in Australia. The New York Times published the news in its American print editions, but not online, while Australian media outlets have tried to sidestep the issue, boldly calling out the court's restrictions while avoiding mention of the underlying news.

Several newspapers published front-page editorials this week. One led with a large-font headline that said: "Censored."

The court, in turn, has been strictly enforcing limits within a common framework.

Suppression orders that completely ban coverage related to continuing sensitive prosecutions have become more frequent in many parts of Australia. It happens more often when there are two related trials in close succession and the goal is obvious: to prevent the risk of prejudice by juries, and to ensure that accusers and the accused can have their cases heard without being undermined at trial or on appeal.

But, international lawyers note, there are other ways to accomplish that. In the United States, the First Amendment prohibits prior restraint on publication in nearly all instances. Courtrooms are rarely closed, and those that are shut mostly involve cases with classified information.

For the most sensitive, dangerous or high-profile cases, such as O. J. Simpson's murder trial, juries are sequestered. They are kept in a hotel away from the internet, television and other media when not in court, and ordered not to discuss the case with anyone.

In Australia, too, there are states — Queensland, for one — that rarely muzzle the media to provide an extra layer of protection for a fair trial. But in Victoria, the location of this particular case, suppression orders have become fairly routine.

Hundreds of cases each year in Victoria are subject to such orders, according to court statistics — a trend that began in the 1990s with dozens of overlapping murder cases involving organized crime. And the scope of these prohibitions tends to be broad. In many cases, they bar all information derived from legal proceedings, including ancillary issues that appear to have little to do with protecting the defendant, like a judge's ruling on challenges to the gag order itself.

Some legal experts in Australia say that such orders reflect a misplaced lack of faith in jurors' ability to reach a fair conclusion without being influenced by coverage or related cases.

"We should trust juries, and we should give clear instructions," said Bruce Baer Arnold, a law professor at the School of Law and Justice at the University of Canberra. He added that this was the standard in the United States, as in most of Australia. "Take the law seriously. Obey instructions. You make your decision on the basis of the argument and the basis of the facts."

Journalists and scholars have also argued that there is another problem with prohibiting publication of facts about such a significant case: the suppression of criticism and accountability.

Several lawyers in Victoria declined to be quoted about the issues raised by this case, even generally, fearing they would run afoul of the judge.

Members of the public who have already spent months in court observing the case's progress have also been silenced, unable to share their conclusions with the world when they are most relevant and likely to be respected.

For now, one judge in an Australian court is altering how the world sees a global figure accused of serious crimes. To preserve a local media blackout, he and the case's lawyers, who have supported the media ban, demand that the rest of the world not publicly debate their competence or the man being prosecuted to ensure, as much as possible, fair treatment in court.

To some, that suppression of information will be seen as a triumph of justice, a noble win for local self-determination and the rule of law.

To others it will be seen as an act that, however well intended, undermines transparency and accountability in a case that much of the world would desperately like to discuss.

LIVIA ALBECK-RIPKA contributed reporting from Melbourne.

CHAPTER 4

Social and Political Issues in the Internet Age

The Internet complicates relations between foreign nations and American companies as well as those between the United States government and its people. Foreign governments can compel companies like Google and Apple to alter their overseas content, causing ethical dilemmas for American tech employees. Internet censorship evolves, but individuals and activists continue to use the web to highlight social and political issues on the digital stage.

A World Map to Outwit Web Censors

BY JOAN OLECK | JUNE 26, 2003

IN RECENT YEARS, Internet censorship has been an increasing focus of scholarly research. At Harvard, the Berkman Center for Internet and Society has identified Web sites — some surprisingly tame — blocked by the governments of Saudi Arabia and China. At the University of Toronto, the Citizen Lab has developed a tool that will enable users to determine whether a Web address is blocked in any of 15 countries.

Now those centers have joined with the Program for Security in International Society at the University of Cambridge in England for what could become the biggest such project yet.

Last month the researchers agreed to collaborate on "mapping" the Internet for such blockages, whether they are imposed by governments, Internet service providers, corporations or even public libraries. The project will involve the enlistment of thousands of volunteers around the world, organizers say.

"The general idea is that when we talk about the World Wide Web, 'world' and 'wide' are no longer to be taken for granted," said Jonathan Zittrain, a Harvard law professor and co-director of the Berkman Center. "Our worry is that barriers are coming up left and right, and they are more likely to come up if they can come up stealthily."

The volunteers will be recruited to lend their personal computers to an effort called distributed computing, allowing the processing of millions of bytes of data while the computers are turned on but not in active use. This approach is already being used by 600,000 volunteers in the four-year-old SETI@home project (setiathome.ssl.berkeley.edu) to analyze radio signals from space for patterns that might indicate extraterrestrial life. Other groups use distributed computing for genetics research and to evaluate drug combinations that might help defeat AIDS, anthrax and cancer.

Mr. Zittrain said the Web censorship project would check millions of Web pages worldwide, asking, "Can I get there from here?" If the blocking of the Web page is related to the Internet service provider's network (as opposed to a computer glitch), that intelligence will be sent "upstream to the mother ship," the home base of the computer program distributed to the volunteers, he said.

The application will also test results from participating computers "next door" (in network terms) to each other. Search engines like Google and Alexa will suggest controversial phrases and popular sites to test.

To assure privacy, volunteers will be able to choose whether to reveal data about the sites they normally frequent, with assurances that their traceable Internet addresses won't be revealed. "We're interested in the neighborhood, not the house," Mr. Zittrain said.

He envisions using the data to create a Web site and world map that would immediately identify new Web barriers, which can arise quickly during times of war and other political stress. "If China decides to block www.uscourts.gov," the Web site of the American federal court system, "the entire world will know it automatically within an hour of the block happening," he said.

After an initial testing phase that is expected to cost about $50,000, the censorship mapping project is to begin operation late this year. (Volunteers can sign up at cyber.law.harvard.edu/filtering/app.) David Anderson, director of the SETI@home project, said the censorship project sounded feasible because it would require less computing time to check Web page access than it does to analyze signals from space.

Mr. Zittrain and his Toronto partner, Ronald J. Deibert, an associate professor of political science who directs the Citizen Lab (www.citizenlab.org), expressed optimism about recruiting volunteers in countries practicing Internet censorship.

"News of this sort of thing gets around by word of digital mouth," Mr. Zittrain said, for example, through mailing lists, chats with friends and e-mail exchanges. "Our worry is having too much demand for the application, not too little."

Identifying barriers in the United States will be part of the project, too. Pennsylvania, for example, allows its attorney general, with a judge's approval, to order Internet service providers to block child pornography sites, a move that Mr. Zittrain described as honorable in intent but an alarming precedent. He said he foresaw efforts to enact laws blocking access to sites that might be engaged in copyright violations or serve as tools for spammers — and expressed concern that in their zeal, lawmakers might block many other sites.

Such moves may gain momentum with the Supreme Court ruling this week upholding the Children's Internet Protection Act, a federal law requiring schools and libraries to install Internet filters on computers used by children or forgo federal financing for Internet access.

With the increasing complexity of global technologies, Dr. Deibert said, "it's up to researchers to interrogate what's going on, and with sophisticated, credible methodologies say exactly what's being blocked, how it's being blocked, why it's being blocked."

Clearing Out the App Stores: Government Censorship Made Easier

COLUMN | BY FARHAD MANJOO | JAN. 18, 2017

THERE'S A NEW FORM of digital censorship sweeping the globe, and it could be the start of something devastating.

In the last few weeks, the Chinese government compelled Apple to remove New York Times apps from the Chinese version of the App Store. Then the Russian government had Apple and Google pull the app for LinkedIn, the professional social network, after the network declined to relocate its data on Russian citizens to servers in that country. Finally, last week, a Chinese regulator asked app stores operating in the country to register with the government, an apparent precursor to wider restrictions on app marketplaces.

These moves may sound incremental, and perhaps not immediately alarming. China has been restricting the web forever, and Russia is no bastion of free speech. So what's so dangerous about blocking apps?

Here's the thing: It's a more effective form of censorship.

Blocking a website is like trying to stop lots of trucks from delivering a banned book; it requires an infrastructure of technical tools (things like China's "Great Firewall"), and enterprising users can often find a way around it. Banning an app from an app store, by contrast, is like shutting down the printing press before the book is ever published. If the app isn't in a country's app store, it effectively doesn't exist. The censorship is nearly total and inescapable.

But that's not the end of this story. The banning of apps highlights a deeper flaw in our modern communications architecture: It's the centralization of information, stupid.

"I think the app store censorship issue is one layer of ice on the surface of the iceberg above the waterline," said Eben Moglen, a professor at Columbia Law School and a leader in the free software movement of

DOUG CHAYKA

activists who have long been warning about the dangers of centrally managed, commercial software.

For more than a decade, we users of digital devices have actively championed an online infrastructure that now looks uniquely vulnerable to the sanctions of despots and others who seek to control information. We flocked to smartphones, app stores, social networks and cloud storage. Publishers like The New York Times are investing in apps and content posted to social networks instead of the comparatively open World Wide Web. Some start-ups now rely exclusively on apps; Snapchat, for instance, exists only as a mobile app.

Compared with older forms of distributing software, apps downloaded from app stores are more convenient for users and often more secure from malware, and they can be more lucrative for creators. But like so much else online now, they risk feeding into mechanisms of central control. In most countries, the Apple and Google app stores are the only places to find apps for devices running their respective operating systems. (There are more choices for Android app stores in China, where Google does not offer its store.)

The internet's earliest boosters considered it a magical tool to liberate people from restrictions on speech. The easy banning of apps suggests that if we let it, the internet could instead become something quite the opposite — one of the most efficient choke points of communication the world has ever seen.

This was not how it was supposed to be. Decentralized communications was once a central promise of the internet. In the 1960s and 1970s, with the world on the brink of nuclear Armageddon, a cadre of academic and military engineers set out to create a communications system that contained no single point of failure or control. The network they came up with, which evolved into the modern internet, connected every machine to every other through many different paths. That way, if any portion of the network were wiped out by an attack, traffic would simply route itself to a new path.

As the threat of nuclear attack diminished and the internet grew, its decentralized design became as much a political selling point as a technical one.

"Ours is a world that is both everywhere and nowhere," the activist John Perry Barlow argued in his 1996 manifesto, "A Declaration of the Independence of Cyberspace." He predicted that because of the internet's everywhere-ness, the world's governments would never be able to lasso the digital realm. The computer scientist and activist John Gilmore told Time magazine in 1993, "The Net interprets censorship as damage and routes around it."

What the creators and early proselytizers of the internet did not foresee was the rapid commercialization of the network. The internet that Mr. Barlow and Mr. Gilmore envisioned was built and maintained by collectives of users; the one that users flocked to was tamed by companies whose very success turned them into some of the largest corporations on the planet.

The internet is now no longer "everywhere and nowhere." Just about all of its economic value is instead connected to two very specific somewheres: the San Francisco Bay Area and Seattle, the homes of Apple, Amazon, Google and Facebook, the four monstrously large companies that own the internet's central information platforms. As these companies began to build ever-larger empires online, they have evolved into convenient choke points — the very points of control that the internet was designed to eliminate.

Like all companies, online companies must offer some level of deference to governments. They obey local and national laws, court orders and national security authorities, and bend to other, less transparent means of coercion. They can fight governments — as Apple did when it battled the F.B.I. over unlocking a terrorist's iPhone last year — but they often must pick their battles and balance their interests. Apple makes a significant fraction of its profits from China. Can it really risk all those billions to protect a handful of apps?

Apple offered this statement in response to my queries on how it decides to take down apps: "For some time now the New York Times app has not been permitted to display content to most users in China, and we have been informed that the app is in violation of local regulations. As a result, the app must be taken down off the China App Store. When this situation changes, the App Store will once again offer the New York Times app for download in China." Google declined to comment.

But Eva Galperin, the director of cybersecurity at the Electronic Frontier Foundation, a digital rights activist organization, said the internet giants were not without leverage in this fight.

"The flip side of that is, is China going to block the entire Apple App Store over a single app?" she asked. Interestingly, the internet giants' hold on every aspect of online life works toward their advantage in battling governments.

"The bigger a company is, the bigger the risk that blocking them will lead to riots in the streets because you have come between people and their pictures of cats," Ms. Galperin said. "Those are the companies that governments are going to be more wary of blocking, and they should be the ones that stand up to government pressure. They have a special responsibility."

Users and app developers who are now at risk of being censored also bear some responsibility. When I asked Mr. Moglen at Columbia about app bans, he was incensed that I didn't recognize The New York Times's own complicity in this story.

The Times, he argued, could have stuck with the old way of publishing news. The company could have declined to create a downloadable app and instead invested all of its engineering resources into making its news available on the web, anonymously. The Times could have refused to profile users for advertising purposes, or to have its articles hosted on Facebook, or to monitor what people read in order to recommend more articles to keep people engaged. In short, The Times could have refused to play the modern digital-publishing game. But like every other publisher, it went along.

"What did you expect would happen?" Mr. Moglen asked. "China didn't have to build a Great Firewall to do this. You all offered them an opportunity to piggyback onto your disrespect for the privacy and integrity and autonomy of your readers and users."

I don't agree with Mr. Moglen that The Times disrespects its readers by offering a news app. (I think it's a very nice app.) But he is right that a lot of people online walked blindly into the no-win position we are in now, where our only recourse against censorship might be the good will of a few giant corporations that control most of the internet.

There has to be some other way. Let's maybe work on finding it.

FARHAD MANJOO writes the State of the Art column for The New York Times.

In Trump Era, Censorship May Start in the Newsroom

COLUMN | BY JIM RUTENBERG | FEB. 17, 2017

THIS IS HOW the muzzling starts: not with a boot on your neck, but with the fear of one that runs so deep that you muzzle yourself.

Maybe it's the story you decide against doing because it's liable to provoke a press-bullying president to put the power of his office behind his attempt to destroy your reputation by falsely calling your journalism "fake."

Maybe it's the line you hold back from your script or your article because it could trigger a federal leak investigation into you and your sources (so, yeah, jail).

Or, maybe it's the commentary you spike because you're a publicly supported news channel and you worry it will cost your station its federal financing.

In that last case, your fear would be existential — a matter of your very survival — and your motivation to self-censor could prove overwhelming.

We no longer have to imagine it. We got a real-life example last week in San Antonio, where a PBS station sat atop the slippery slope toward censorship and then promptly started down it.

It's a single television station in a single state in a very big country. And the right thing ultimately happened. But only after a very wrong thing happened.

The editorial misfire bears retelling because it showed the most likely way that the new administration's attempts to shut down the free press could succeed, just as it shows how those attempts can be stopped.

The story began with a Jan. 24 speech that Representative Lamar Smith, Republican of Texas, gave on the House floor regarding what he described as the unfair way the national media was covering President Trump. He said for instance that the media ignored highs in consumer confidence, which of course it did not. And he ended with an admonition for his constituents: "Better to get your news directly from the president. In fact, it might be the only way to get the unvarnished truth."

His remarks caught the notice, and the ire, of a longtime San Antonio-area journalist and commentator, Rick Casey, who hosts a weekly public affairs program "Texas Week" on KLRN. He ends each week's show with his own commentary, which also runs in The San Antonio Express-News.

Mr. Casey has been able to work for "40 years as a professional smart ass," he told me, because "I'm not really a bomb thrower — I've watched politicians for so many years that I know how to be strong about something without being unfriendly."

But Mr. Smith's comments bothered him enough that he wrote up a stemwinder of a closing commentary. "Smith's proposal is quite innovative for America," it went. "We've never really tried getting all our news from our top elected official. It has been tried elsewhere, however. North Korea comes to mind."

All set to go, the commentary was mentioned in a Facebook promotion for the show, which in turn caught the eye of Mr. Smith's office, which called the station to inquire about the segment.

Forty minutes before the show aired, the station's president and chief executive, Arthur Rojas Emerson, left a message for Mr. Casey saying he was pulling the commentary and replacing it with an older one. Mr. Casey told me he missed the call, but saw what happened with his own eyes.

At a meeting the next Monday, Mr. Casey said, Mr. Emerson expressed concern "that the Corporation for Public Broadcasting was under attack and that this would add to it." The Corporation for Public Broadcasting provides financing for public stations, including KLRN, and Mr. Trump's election has heightened fears that its financing will be cut.

It also happens that Mr. Emerson had left journalism for several years to run his own advertising firm and that Mr. Smith had at one point been a client.

JOSH HUSKIN FOR THE NEW YORK TIMES

Rick Casey, the host of a weekly public affairs program on a small television station in Texas, recently fashioned a stinging commentary on remarks by Representative Lamar Smith that was pulled shortly before it was to air. The station later reversed itself.

Mr. Casey says he asked Mr. Emerson if he'd be willing to come on the program and discuss it all, but Mr. Emerson declined. And that seemed to be that.

But as we're learning this year, journalism has a safety net in the people who appreciate it, and the people who work in it.

First, when Mr. Casey's commentary ran as planned in The San Antonio Express-News, astute readers noticed it was different than the previous night's televised commentary. The story of what happened began traveling around San Antonio journalism circles, making its way to the Express-News columnist Gilbert Garcia, who shared the details last Friday.

Another titan of Texas journalism, Evan Smith, who co-founded The Texas Tribune and regularly appears on Mr. Casey's program, noticed Mr. Garcia's column while he was in Washington. "I had a hot coffee in my hand and I came very close to dropping it," Mr. Smith told me. "Holding people accountable in public life is so fundamentally important that this idea that somehow we're going to stop doing that because we're worried about what the government's going to do to us, I so unbelievably reject that."

As it happened, Evan Smith was in Washington for a meeting of the PBS national board, on which he sits, and "I certainly got into the board room and talked to people in the system." He also called Mr. Emerson, and told him "I didn't see why The Tribune or I should continue to be associated with this show or this station."

By late last week, Mr. Emerson had agreed to let Mr. Casey's original segment run this Friday, as long as it included a new "commentary" label that will run with his opinion segments.

When I caught up with Mr. Emerson this week he acknowledged making "a mistake" that should not tarnish a career spent mostly in broadcast news, starting in a $1.25-an-hour job as a cameraman. "I had to make a decision in what was about 20 minutes," he said.

He acknowledged that "clearly we always worry about funding for public television," but said that wasn't the "principal reason" for his decision to hold back the commentary. "We have to protect the neutrality of the station — somebody could have looked at it as slander," he said. The "commentary" label, he said, would take care of it.

Mr. Casey is satisfied with the result. But he acknowledged that it was a close call and that he was uniquely qualified to push back in a way others might not be. "I'm lucky to be in the position of being 70 years old, and not in the position of being 45," he said, meaning that job security was not the same issue. "There's no level of heroism here."

In a week in which Congress is calling for a leak investigation into stories in The Washington Post, The New York Times and CNN that led to Michael T. Flynn's forced resignation as national security adviser, heroism is what's called for. Hopefully there's enough of it to go around.

ZACH WICHTER contributed research.

JIM RUTENBERG writes the Mediator column for The New York Times.

How Important Is Freedom of the Press?

BY NATALIE PROULX | MAY 4, 2018

Editor's Note: This article is part of The New York Times's Learning Network, which offers opportunities for teaching and learning with The Times.

IN HONOR OF World Press Freedom Day on May 3, The New York Times tweeted:

In honor of #WorldPressFreedomDay, @nytimes is joining other news orgs to encourage readers to consume news from multiple outlets #ReadMoreListenMore

— NYTimes Communications (@NYTimesPR) May 3, 2018

What is your reaction to the tweet? Do you agree with its message? Why or why not?

Do you get news from multiple sources? Do you think doing so is important?

In "Turkish Cartoonist Wins Prize on World Press Freedom Day," Reuters reports:

A Turkish caricaturist facing more than three years in jail won the International Press Drawing Prize on Thursday, an award given every two years to leading cartoonists, especially those working under authoritarian regimes.

Musa Kart of the opposition newspaper Cumhuriyet was one of 14 staff handed sentences last month ranging from 2 1/2 to 7 1/2 years on charges of supporting Fethullah Gulen, the U.S.-based Muslim cleric that Ankara blames for a 2016 attempted coup. They have denied the charges.

Kart, 64, was sentenced to three years and nine months and is banned from travel pending his appeal. After the coup attempt, he spent nine months in prison.

"My beloved newspaper is currently surrounded by those who are uncomfortable with its journalism and want to silence it completely by

threatening heavy punishments," Kart said in a message read out by his daughter, Seran Uney, to a ceremony in Geneva on Thursday, marking World Press Freedom Day.

The staff of the Istanbul newspaper, long seen as a thorn in the side of President Tayyip Erdogan, is one of the few remaining voices critical of the government.

The jury of the Cartooning for Peace Foundation includes cartoonists Jean Plantu of France and Patrick Chappatte of Switzerland, and Ken Roth, executive director of Human Rights Watch.

They make the award based on cartoonists' "approach and commitment … especially if their cartoons were published in a political context of repression and censorship."

In an Opinion essay from May 6, 2017, Carol Giacomo gives more background on the conflict in Turkey and speaks to its implications for a free press:

With some 163 of their fellow journalists in jail, the men and women of Turkey's news media are understandably fearful. Many of those who avoided prison as part of President Recep Tayyip Erdogan's sweeping crackdown on alleged enemies after a July coup attempt have lost their jobs at media outlets taken over by Mr. Erdogan's cronies. Some of those still working censor themselves in self-defense.

In such an environment, even getting together to talk about challenges to the fast-fading press freedoms in Turkey's ever-shrinking democracy is an act of courage. That happened on Wednesday when Platform24, an Istanbul-based nonprofit fighting for journalists' right to do their jobs, held an event to celebrate World Press Freedom Day with a lecture honoring the late Mehmet Ali Birand, one of the country's most admired journalists. Given Mr. Erdogan's tendency for retaliation, the Swedish consul general, Therese Hyden, also deserves credit for hosting the event.

The mood this year, however, was anything but celebratory, and for obvious reasons. Under Mr. Erdogan's authoritarian rule, not just an independent press but many rights and freedoms have sharply deteriorated. Instead, the mood was somber as Platform24's staff performed a kind of dirge, reading the names of imprisoned colleagues one by one.

"We want them to know, we want their families to know, we want their readers and audiences to know, and we want the government to

know that they are not alone," said Yasemin Congar, one of Platform24's founders.

"Journalism is not a crime," she added.

Students:

— In your opinion, what is the purpose of journalism? What is its role in society? How does it serve individuals?

— What values and ideals do you think quality journalism should uphold and defend and why?

— How important is it for a country — and the world — to have a free press? Why do you think so?

— Are there any topics or opinions that you think should be censored in the press? Or should journalists have absolute freedom of speech?

— Ms. Giacomo writes that President Trump has become a "threat … to the free press in America with relentless attempts to delegitimize any reputable media outlet that dared criticize him." What do you think of this statement? Should high-powered politicians and world leaders be able to denounce media they disagree with? Why or why not?

Google Employees Protest Secret Work on Censored Search Engine for China

BY KATE CONGER AND DAISUKE WAKABAYASHI | AUG. 16, 2018

HUNDREDS OF GOOGLE employees, upset at the company's decision to secretly build a censored version of its search engine for China, have signed a letter demanding more transparency to understand the ethical consequences of their work.

In the letter, which was obtained by The New York Times, employees wrote that the project and Google's apparent willingness to abide by China's censorship requirements "raise urgent moral and ethical issues." They added, "Currently we do not have the information required to make ethically-informed decisions about our work, our projects, and our employment."

The letter is circulating on Google's internal communication systems and is signed by about 1,400 employees, according to three people familiar with the document, who were not authorized to speak publicly.

The internal activism presents another obstacle for Google's potential return to China eight years after the company publicly withdrew from the country in protest of censorship and government hacking. China has the world's largest internet audience but has frustrated American tech giants with content restrictions or outright blockages of services including Facebook and Instagram.

It is also the latest example of how Google's outspoken work force has agitated for changes to strategy. In April, the internet company's employees spoke out against its involvement in a Pentagon program that uses artificial intelligence to improve weaponry. By June, Google had said it would not renew a contract with the Pentagon for A.I. work.

Google's interest in bringing search back to China came to the forefront earlier this month, when reports surfaced that the company was working on a search app that restricts content banned by Beijing.

The project, known internally as Dragonfly, was developed largely in secret, prompting outrage among employees who worried they had been unwittingly working on technology that would help China withhold information from its citizens.

"We urgently need more transparency, a seat at the table, and a commitment to clear and open processes: Google employees need to know what we're building," the letter said.

The letter also called on Google to allow employees to participate in ethical reviews of the company's products, to appoint external representatives to ensure transparency and to publish an ethical assessment of controversial projects. The document referred to the situation as a code yellow, a process used in engineering to address critical problems that impact several teams.

Google declined to comment on the letter. It has said in the past that it will not comment on Dragonfly or "speculation about future plans."

Late on Thursday, employees pressed Google's chief executive, Sundar Pichai, and other management about Dragonfly at a weekly staff meeting. As of late Wednesday, one of the top questions on an internal software system called Dory, which lets employees vote for the queries that executives should answer at the meeting, asked whether Google had lost its ethical compass, said people who had reviewed the questions. Other questions on Dory asked directly about the Dragonfly project and specific information that may be censored by the Chinese government, such as air pollution data.

"If we were to do our mission well, we are to think seriously about how to do more in China," Mr. Pichai said in the staff meeting, audio of which was obtained by The Times. "That said, we are not close to launching a search product in China."

Mr. Pichai and Sergey Brin, a co-founder of Google, stopped answering questions about Dragonfly after seeing their answers posted on Twitter.

This week's staff meeting was the first opportunity for Google's work force to ask executives about Dragonfly, because the meeting was not held last week. The absence of a gathering — the result of a regularly scheduled break in the summer, according to a company spokesman, Rob Shilkin — led to fears among employees that leadership was becoming less transparent following several controversies over Google's government work.

Google has traditionally been more responsive to employee concerns and more transparent about future projects and inner workings than other major technology companies, inviting questions from workers at its staff meetings and encouraging internal debate.

The internal dissent over Dragonfly comes on the heels of the employee protests over Google's involvement in the Pentagon project to use artificial intelligence. After Google said it would not renew its contract with the Pentagon, it unveiled a series of ethical principles governing its use of A.I.

In those principles, Google publicly committed to use A.I. only in "socially beneficial" ways that would not cause harm and promised to develop its capabilities in accordance with human rights law. Some employees have raised concerns that helping China suppress the free flow of information would violate these new principles.

In 2010, Google said it had discovered that Chinese hackers had attacked the company's corporate infrastructure in an attempt to access the Gmail accounts of human rights activists. The attack, combined with government censorship, propelled Google to pull its search engine from the country.

The exit from China was a seminal moment for the company — a symbol of its uncompromising idealism captured by Google's unofficial motto of "Don't Be Evil." At the time, Chinese internet users marked the loss of Google's search engine by laying flowers at the company's Beijing offices in what became known as an "illegal flower tribute." A possible re-entry to China, according to current and former employees, is a sign of a more mature and pragmatic company.

Google has maintained a significant presence in China even though its flagship services are not accessible in the country. Last year,

Google announced plans for a research center in China focused on artificial intelligence. And it has introduced translation and file management apps for the Chinese market. Google now has more than 700 employees in China.

Google's work on Dragonfly is not a guarantee that its search engine will be welcomed back to China. The government would have to approve its return and it has kept American technology firms like Facebook at arm's length, opting instead to work closely with homegrown internet behemoths.

Some employees are in favor of re-entering China, arguing that exiting the country in protest of censorship has done little to pressure Beijing to change its position while it has made Google nonessential among the world's largest base of internet users.

When Google pulled out of China in 2010, Mr. Brin said it objected to the country's "totalitarian" policies when it came to censorship, political speech and internet communications. If anything, China has only tightened its controls in the last eight years — leaving the company in a bind for how to justify its return.

"You can never satisfy a censor, particularly the ones in China," said Charles Mok, member of the Hong Kong Legislative Council who advocates and represents the information technology sector and who is affiliated with the territory's democratic camp.

Google is probably facing intense pressure to introduce more of its products in China, Mr. Mok said, but added that the company would lend legitimacy to government censorship if it debuted a censored search product in China.

"Then the Chinese government can say, 'Google is O.K. with it, too,' " he said.

The Dangers of Digital Activism

OPINION | BY MANAL AL-SHARIF | SEPT. 16, 2018

AS A SAUDI ARABIAN WOMAN who has lived most of her life under one of the last surviving absolute monarchies in the world, the closest I have come to experiencing democracy has been in challenging the status quo through my tweets.

For activists and citizen journalists in the Arab world, social media has become a powerful way to express dissent, to disrupt and to organize. Digital activism, however, comes at a high price: The very tools we use for our cause can be — and have been — used to undermine us.

While social media platforms were designed as a way to connect people online, activists used them as technological tools of liberation, devising creative hacks to defy state censorship, connect with like-minded people, mobilize the masses, influence public opinion, push for social change and ignite revolutions. With these opportunities came risks: The more we posted and engaged, the more vulnerable we became, as our aggregated data was weaponized against us. Over time, such data can be used to build an accurate picture not only of users' preferences, likes and behaviors, but also of their beliefs, political views and intimate personal details; things that even their family and friends may not know about them.

For a fee, social media platforms offer access to users' information via internally developed analytical tools. I'm not talking about the sale of information to advertising agencies, whose goal is to promote a client's products. This is annoying, but only minimally harmful. I'm talking about clients with the clear intention of harming and persecuting users: state authorities, intelligence agencies and fundamentalist religious groups.

As more people have joined social media, disrupting the traditional ways that information and content are generated and shared (even though traditional media in the Middle East is largely controlled by governments and a small number of powerful and influential corporations), so too have ill-intentioned groups focused on generating misinformation and spreading hate speech, sectarianism and even terrorism.

The use of social media is more prevalent than ever in Saudi Arabia. The kingdom has the largest number of active Twitter users and the largest number of generated tweets across the Middle East and North Africa, according to the 2017 Arab Social Media Report. And according to a report conducted by two Saudi researchers at Rutgers University, more than 40 percent of the 6.3 million Saudis on Twitter in 2016 were women. Many of the accounts were anonymous; users pressed for social change and greater gender equality.

As an influencer in the Saudi Arabian Twittersphere, I don't have the luxury of hiding behind my anonymity. In late 2017, when we heard rumors that Gulf Cooperation Council governments had decided to use our old tweets to build cases against us, many activists started taking measures to delete them.

Twitter, however, had different ideas. As of February, Twitter has started offering a service that enables people to access archives of its users' tweets going all the way back to 2006. Anyone can request access to these archives for as cheaply as $99 per month. Access to these archives provides an unprecedented opportunity for surveillance, or "dataveillance," and intimidation by authoritarian regimes. (Bear in mind that just weeks before the Saudi ban on women drivers was lifted, some of the very women and men who campaigned for it were detained by the government.)

Even the West has had to contend with the aftermath of attacks on the democratic process that employ social media. According to NBC News, Twitter deleted some 200,000 troll tweets in 2018 that had been tracked to a Kremlin-based propaganda machine, which saturated Twitter with false and inflammatory news leading up to the 2016 United States presidential election. Of course, the news came too late.

Trolling and using fake accounts on Twitter are not new tactics. They have even been used against me on a personal level. Attacks on me have ranged from pro-government and fundamentalist groups spreading fake news and rumors about me (I was once reported killed in a car accident, which made international headlines) to the vicious smearing of the #Women2Drive campaign, a right-to-drive movement for women in Saudi Arabia that I co-founded in 2011. Despite the offending accounts being reported countless times, Twitter took no action.

It has been happening on a larger scale, too. In September 2017, during a time of high tension between Qatar and Saudi Arabia, the parent company of Snapchat bowed to pressure from government officials and removed the Al Jazeera network, which is funded by Qatar, from its platform in Saudi Arabia.

As the activist and computer engineer Wael Ghonim said: "The Arab Spring revealed social media's greatest potential, but it also exposed its greatest shortcomings. The same tool that united us to topple dictators eventually tore us apart." While social media was useful in sparking movements demanding political and societal reforms in 2011, we failed to maintain that momentum, in part because the platforms we have been using are ultimately driven by profit.

The time is ripe for disruption of a different sort. People seeking technological liberation are moving toward alternative social media platforms like Crabgrass, Mastodon and Diaspora, which allow social connectivity with an additional layer of privacy and security. We need platforms that are open, decentralized and don't archive and sell users' information to the highest bidder. This way, people can participate based on the merits of their content, not on how much they pay for views.

Unless social media giants take real steps toward the fair and safe use of their platforms, we activists will move on to the next best thing — one that allows us to share our dreams without placing us on the auction block.

MANAL AL-SHARIF, co-founder and leader of the #Women2Drive movement and founder and CEO of Women2Hack Academy, is author of the memoir "Daring to Drive: A Saudi Woman's Awakening."

There May Soon Be Three Internets. America's Won't Necessarily Be the Best.

EDITORIAL | BY THE NEW YORK TIMES | OCT. 15, 2018

A breakup of the web grants privacy, security and freedom to some, and not so much to others.

The editorial board represents the opinions of the board, its editor and the publisher. It is separate from the newsroom and the Op-Ed section.

IN SEPTEMBER, ERIC SCHMIDT, the former Google chief executive and Alphabet chairman, said that in the next 10 to 15 years, the internet would most likely be split in two — one internet led by China and one internet led by the United States.

Mr. Schmidt, speaking at a private event hosted by a venture capital firm, did not seem to seriously entertain the possibility that the internet would remain global. He's correct to rule out that possibility — if anything, the flaw in Mr. Schmidt's thinking is that he too quickly dismisses the European internet that is coalescing around the European Union's ever-heightening regulation of technology platforms. All signs point to a future with three internets.

The received wisdom was once that a unified, unbounded web promoted democracy through the free flow of information. Things don't seem quite so simple anymore. China's tight control of the internet within its borders continues to tamp down talk of democracy, and an increasingly sophisticated system of digital surveillance plays a major role in human rights abuses, such as the persecution of the Uighurs. We've also seen the dark side to connecting people to one another — as illustrated by how misinformation on social media played a significant role in the violence in Myanmar.

There's a world of difference between the European Union's

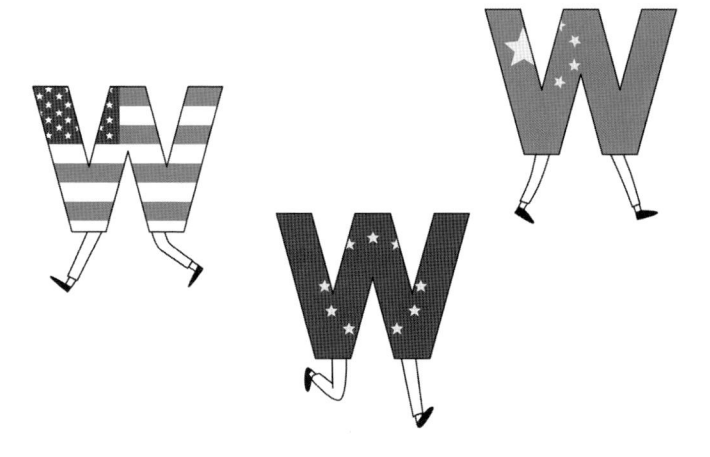

ROSE WONG

General Data Protection Regulation, known commonly as G.D.P.R., and China's technologically enforced censorship regime, often dubbed "the Great Firewall." But all three spheres — Europe, America and China — are generating sets of rules, regulations and norms that are beginning to rub up against one another. What's more, the actual physical location of data has increasingly become separated by region, with data confined to data centers inside the borders of countries with data localization laws.

The information superhighway cracks apart more easily when so much of it depends on privately owned infrastructure. An error at Amazon Web Services created losses of service across the web in 2017; a storm disrupting a data center in Northern Virginia created similar failures in 2012. These were unintentional blackouts; the corporate custodians of the internet have it within their power to do far more. Of course, nobody wants to turn off the internet completely — that wouldn't make anyone money. But when a single company with huge market share chooses to comply with a law — or more worryingly, a mere suggestion from the authorities — a large chunk of the internet ends up falling in line.

The power of a handful of platforms and services combined with the dismal state of international cooperation across the world pushes us closer and closer to a splintered internet. Meanwhile, American companies that once implicitly pushed democratic values abroad are more reticent to take a stand.

In 2010, Google shut down its operations in China after it was revealed that the Chinese government had been hacking the Gmail accounts of dissidents and surveilling them through the search engine. "At some point you have to stand back and challenge this and say, this goes beyond the line of what we're comfortable with, and adopt that for moral reasons," said Sergey Brin, a Google co-founder, in an interview with Der Spiegel at the time.

But eight years later, Google is working on a search engine for China known as Dragonfly. Its launch will be conditional on the approval of Chinese officials and will therefore comply with stringent censorship requirements. An internal memo written by one of the engineers on the project described surveillance capabilities built into the engine — namely by requiring users to log in and then tracking their browsing histories. This data will be accessible by an unnamed Chinese partner, presumably the government.

Google says all features are speculative and no decision has been made on whether to launch Dragonfly, but a leaked transcript of a meeting inside Google later acquired by The Intercept, a news site, contradicts that line. In the transcript, Google's head of search, Ben Gomes, is quoted as saying that it hoped to launch within six to nine months, although the unstable American-China relationship makes it difficult to predict when or even whether the Chinese government will give the go-ahead. "There is a huge binary difference between being launched and not launched," said Mr. Gomes. "And so we want to be careful that we don't miss that window if it ever comes."

Internet censorship and surveillance were once hallmarks of

oppressive governments — with Egypt, Iran and China being prime examples. It's since become clear that secretive digital surveillance isn't just the domain of anti-democratic forces. The Snowden revelations in 2013 knocked the United States off its high horse, and may have pushed the technology industry into an increasingly agnostic outlook on human rights. Its relationship with the government isn't improving, either, when the industry is being hammered by the Trump administration's continuing trade wars. (This month, Vice President Mike Pence condemned Dragonfly as part of a longer, confrontational speech accusing China of "economic aggression.")

As governments push toward a splintered internet, American corporations do little to counteract Balkanization and instead do whatever is necessary to expand their operations. If the future of the internet is a tripartite cold war, Silicon Valley wants to be making money in all three of those worlds.

Part of the rationalization is that whether or not American companies get in on the action, a homegrown company will readily enact the kind of censorship and surveillance that its government requires. (Indeed, if Google launches in China, it has an uphill battle to fight against Baidu, the entrenched, government-endorsed Chinese search engine.)

What this future will bring for Europe and the United States is not clear. Mr. Gomes's leaked speech from inside Google sounded almost dystopian at times. "This is a world none of us have ever lived in before," Mr. Gomes told employees. "All I am saying, we have built a set of hacks, and we have kept them." He seemed to hint at scenarios the tech sector had never imagined before. The world may be a very different place since the election of Donald Trump, but it's still hard to imagine that what's deployed in China will ever be deployed at home. Yet even the best possible version of the disaggregated web has serious — though still uncertain — implications for a global future: What sorts of ideas and speech will become bounded by borders? What will an increasingly disconnected world do to the spread of innovation and to scientific progress? What will consumer protections around privacy and security look like as the internets diverge? And would the partitioning of the internet precipitate a slowing, or even a reversal, of globalization?

A chillier relationship with Europe and increasing hostilities with China spur on the trend toward Balkanization — and vice versa, creating a feedback loop. If things continue along this path, the next decade may see the internet relegated to little more than just another front on the new cold war.

The Poison on Facebook and Twitter Is Still Spreading

EDITORIAL | BY THE NEW YORK TIMES | OCT. 19, 2018

Social platforms have a responsibility to address misinformation as a systemic problem, instead of reacting to case after case.

The editorial board represents the opinions of the board, its editor and the publisher. It is separate from the newsroom and the Op-Ed section.

A NETWORK OF FACEBOOK troll accounts operated by the Myanmar military parrots hateful rhetoric against Rohingya Muslims. Viral misinformation runs rampant on WhatsApp in Brazil, even as marketing firms there buy databases of phone numbers in order to spam voters with right-wing messaging. Homegrown campaigns spread partisan lies in the United States.

The public knows about each of these incitements because of reporting by news organizations. Social media misinformation is becoming a newsroom beat in and of itself, as journalists find themselves acting as unpaid content moderators for these platforms.

It's not just reporters, either. Academic researchers and self-taught vigilantes alike scour through networks of misinformation on social media platforms, their findings prompting — or sometimes, failing to prompt — the takedown of propaganda.

It's the latest iteration of a journalistic cottage industry that started out by simply comparing and contrasting questionable moderation decisions — the censorship of a legitimate news article, perhaps, or an example of terrorist propaganda left untouched. Over time, the stakes have become greater and greater. Once upon a time, the big Facebook censorship controversy was the banning of female nipples in photos. That feels like a idyllic bygone era never to return.

The internet platforms will always make some mistakes, and it's not fair to expect otherwise. And the task before Facebook, YouTube,

ROSE WONG

Twitter, Instagram and others is admittedly herculean. No one can screen everything in the fire hose of content produced by users. Even if a platform makes the right call on 99 percent of its content, the remaining 1 percent can still be millions upon millions of postings. The platforms are due some forgiveness in this respect.

It's increasingly clear, however, that at this stage of the internet's evolution, content moderation can no longer be reduced to individual postings viewed in isolation and out of context. The problem is systemic, currently manifested in the form of coordinated campaigns both foreign and homegrown. While Facebook and Twitter have been making strides toward proactively staving off dubious influence campaigns, a tired old pattern is re-emerging — journalists and researchers find a problem, the platform reacts and the whole cycle begins anew. The merry-go-round spins yet again.

This week, a question from The New York Times prompted Facebook to take down a network of accounts linked to the Myanmar military. Although Facebook was already aware of the problem in general, the request for comment from The Times flagged specific instances of "seemingly independent entertainment, beauty and informational pages" that were tied to a military operation that sowed the internet with anti-Rohingya sentiment.

The week before, The Times found a number of suspicious pages spreading viral misinformation about Christine Blasey Ford, the woman who has accused Brett Kavanaugh of assault. After The Times showed Facebook some of those pages, the company said it had already been looking into the issue. Facebook took down the pages flagged by The Times, but similar pages that hadn't yet been shown to the company stayed up.

It's not just The Times, and it's not just Facebook. Again and again, the act of reporting out a story gets reduced to outsourced content moderation.

"We all know that feeling," says Charlie Warzel, a reporter at BuzzFeed who's written about everything from viral misinformation on Twitter to exploitative child content on YouTube. "You flag a flagrant violation of terms of service and send out a request for comment. And you're just sitting there refreshing, and then you see it come down — and afterward you get this boilerplate reply via email." Mr. Warzel says his inbox is full of messages from people begging him to intercede with the platforms on their behalf — sometimes because they have been censored unfairly, sometimes because they want to point to disturbing content they believe should be taken offline.

Journalists are not in the business of resolving disputes for Facebook and Twitter. But disgruntled users might feel that they have a better chance of being listened to by a reporter than by someone who is actually paid to resolve user complaints.

Of course, it would be far worse if a company refused to patch a problem that journalists have uncovered. But at the same time, muckraking isn't meant to fix the system one isolated instance at a time. Imagine if Nellie Bly had to infiltrate the same asylum over and over again, with each investigation prompting a single incremental change, like the removal of one abusive nurse.

The work of journalists is taken for granted, both implicitly and explicitly. In August, the Twitter CEO, Jack Dorsey, took to his own platform to defend his company's decision to keep Alex Jones online. "Accounts like Jones' can often sensationalize issues and spread unsubstantiated rumors, so it's critical journalists document, validate, and refute such information directly so people can form their own opinions," he said. "This is what serves the public conversation best." But journalists and outside researchers do not have access to the wealth of data available internally to companies like Twitter and Facebook.

The companies have all the tools at their disposal and a profound responsibility to find exactly what journalists find — and yet, clearly, they don't. The role that outsiders currently play, as consumer advocates and content screeners, can easily be filled in-house. And unlike journalists, companies have the power to change the very incentives that keep producing these troubling online phenomena.

The reliance on journalists' time is particularly paradoxical given the damage that the tech companies are doing to the media industry. Small changes to how Facebook organizes its News Feed can radically change a news organization's bottom line — layoffs and hiring sprees are spurred on by the whims of the algorithm. Even as the companies draw on journalistic resources to make their products better, the hegemony of Google and Facebook over digital advertising — estimated by some to be a combined 85 percent of the market — is strangling journalism.

But throwing light on the coordinated misinformation campaigns flaring up all around us is a matter that is much bigger than the death of print — it's essential to democracy. It can change the course of elections and genocides. Social media platforms are doing society no favors by relying on journalists to leach the poison from their sites. Because none of this is sustainable — and we definitely don't want to find out what happens when the merry-go-round stops working.

The Problem With Banning Pornography on Tumblr

OPINION | BY JESSICA POWELL | DEC. 6, 2018

The decision has taken away an essential platform for some women and members of the L.G.B.T.Q. community.

THIS WEEK, THE SOCIAL networking site Tumblr banned the very thing that drove many people to its site: adult content. Many cheered that Tumblr had finally caught up with the times, echoing anti-pornography policies adopted by Facebook, YouTube, Instagram and others. But there was another set of voices you might not have heard — the voices of women and the L.G.B.T.Q. community — who pointed out that this change will destroy a safe space for self-expression, discovery and connection.

While we can get hung up on debating what kind of content should or shouldn't be allowed on a particular platform, none of that alters an equally important but less-visible problem: When tech companies tackle large-scale problems with large-scale solutions, underrepresented groups are often further marginalized as a result.

The change in Tumblr policy seems to have been born from a reasonable concern. In this case, child pornography was discovered on the platform. There is, of course, a big difference between child pornography and adult content, but Tumblr may have decided that the only way to effectively filter out the former was to eradicate the latter. Or it may simply have decided that moderating pornography was too expensive. Whatever the case, Tumblr said that it was all in favor of creative expression and deep community, but that it would ban all adult content — specifically, all "images, videos, or GIFs that show real-life human genitals or female-presenting nipples," and any content depicting sex acts.

This is not the first time a social media or blog platform has banned adult content. Twitter, Facebook, and many other platforms all prohibit pornography. But in the United States, we seem to ignore public debate about the censorship of sex and the human body, reflecting the American tendency to get more offended by the sight of a female-presenting nipple than by guns, hate speech or violence.

While all efforts must be made to eradicate illegal content on Tumblr, it's important to acknowledge that underrepresented groups have carved out safe spaces on the platform. Tumblr has thrived in part thanks to its unique identity as a place for adult content. Young women dominate the platform, and many turn to it as a place to find more empowering, female-centric takes on pornography and the female body. On Tumblr, one could find pages dedicated to celebrating bodies of all types, could browse sophisticated fetish images curated from a female perspective, and could find GIFs and videos that — unlike most mainstream pornography sites — depict female pleasure.

Some of Tumblr's users spoke out against the company's decision, like Vex Ashley, a performer who makes pornography, who tweeted, "I can't tell you how important it is for work about and with sex to have space to exist next to work about every other part of human experience." She used Tumblr to socialize and network, and as a place to share videos, images and behind-the-scenes photos.

Similarly, many in the L.G.B.T.Q. community have said the adult content on Tumblr provided a space to connect with those with similar interests and to explore sexuality without judgment.

"If not for tumblr i probably wouldnt have realized or even accepted the possibility of me being gay/trans," said one trans Tumblr user (who goes by the Twitter handle of @nonsensecodons).

The problem isn't just about agreeing on what kind of content to allow on a platform, or whether adult content is a positive or negative force in society. It's also that tech companies like Tumblr make statements about wanting to be a positive place for diverse communities, all the while not truly understanding these communities and allowing their algorithms to target their adult content.

To be fair, it is a hard nut to crack. Platforms with millions of users need algorithmic solutions to solve issues like content regulation at scale. The problem is, machines are not yet very good at nuance. Can Tumblr's artificial intelligence tell the difference between a curated page of visual erotica and violent sexual imagery the same way a trained human could? Probably not. There are many examples of Tumblr's A.I. making mistakes, in which non-explicit fan art, pictures of a person's hands, a cartoon image of two men kissing and a vigorous, sweaty game of Ping-Pong set off the platform's A.I. filters. Tumblr has said there will be an appeals process staffed by real live humans, but the human part seems like an afterthought, as it so often does with tech companies.

While there is no perfect solution, there are many steps Tumblr could take if it truly wanted to support these communities. A more nuanced policy could be developed and then implemented through greater short-term investment in more human moderation and long-term investment in A.I.

Without the ability to judge nuance at scale and to distinguish between empowering versus damaging content, Tumblr has adopted a policy that destroys communities who are among its greatest fans. It is a lesson all tech companies should keep in mind when they are debating policy changes: When you cast a wide net, you may sacrifice a group you never intended to hurt.

JESSICA POWELL is the former head of communications for Google and the author of "The Big Disruption: A Totally Fictional but Essentially True Silicon Valley Story."

CHAPTER 5

Case Studies in Russia, China and Saudi Arabia

In the digital age, some countries take extreme steps to control the information and platforms their people have access to. Russia, China and Saudi Arabia monitor not only the information their private citizens consume but also that of other nations around the globe. While public opinion on censorship may vary in each country, there can be dangerous consequences for those a government wishes to censor: The case of journalist Jamal Khashoggi's assassination in 2018 highlights the extreme lengths a government may go to in order to silence dissent.

Who Likes Web Censorship? (Ask Putin.)

ANALYSIS | BY MARJORIE CONNELLY | APRIL 22, 2014

IF YOU WANT to explore how Russians' attitudes toward an authoritarian government may be different from attitudes elsewhere, one place to look is how they think about censorship and freedom on the web.

For the most part, using the Internet causes people to become more strongly in favor of Internet freedom.

People in countries where web access approaches ubiquity are overwhelmingly in favor of being able to use the web without govern-

DENIS SINYAKOV/AFP/GETTY IMAGES

Russian President Vladimir Putin on a computer screen in an internet cafe in Moscow.

ment oversight. This tends to hold true in both affluent countries and more impoverished ones.

More than half of the people in Argentina, Chile, Lebanon and Venezuela have web access, for instance, and 80 percent or more of people in each of those countries say people should "have access to the Internet without government censorship," according to Pew Research Center polls taken last spring. In Senegal, on the other hand, where about a third of people have web access, only about 60 percent favor web freedom.

Russia is an exception. Internet access in Russia is similar to access in Argentina and Chile, but attitudes toward freedom are similar to those in Senegal. Even though most Russians use the web, many are comfortable with web censorship.

'They Want to Block Our Future': Thousands Protest Russia's Internet Censorship

BY NEIL MACFARQUHAR | APRIL 30, 2018

MOSCOW — A demonstration in Moscow against the Russian government's effort to block the messaging app Telegram quickly morphed on Monday into a protest against President Vladimir V. Putin, with thousands of participants chanting against the Kremlin's increasingly restrictive bent.

The key demand of the rally, with the hashtag #DigitalResistance, was that the Russian internet remain free from government censorship.

"Do you believe that Putin knows about blocking Telegram?" one speaker, Sergei Smirnov, editor in chief of Mediazona, an online news service, asked the crowd. "Is he to blame for blocking Telegram?"

The crowd responded with a resounding "Yes!" to both questions.

"Telegram is just the first step," Mr. Smirnov continued. "If they block Telegram, it will be worse later. They will block everything. They want to block our future and the future of our children."

The rally comes two weeks after Roskomnadzor, the official internet watchdog, began its bumbling effort to shut down Telegram by blocking what the regulator said was some 18 million I.P. addresses.

The F.S.B., the K.G.B.'s successor agency, went to court to obtain the order to block the app after Pavel V. Durov, Telegram's inventor, a Russian who lives in exile, declined to provide the security agency with the means to decrypt messages. The F.S.B. said it needed to be able to read the messages to thwart terrorist attacks.

The effort to close Telegram has knocked out countless other sites, including some top websites, like Yandex and Vkontakte, the Russian equivalents of Google and Facebook. Although the shutdowns were brief, those companies did not hide their pique.

"We do not consider this situation to be acceptable," Yandex said in a statement. "The Russian market can develop only in conditions of open competition."

The effort has provoked anger and frustration far beyond the habitual supporters of the political opposition, especially in the business sector, where the collateral damage continues to hurt the bottom line. There has been a flood of complaints on Twitter and elsewhere that the government "broke the internet."

"A large number of people are aware of the situation and they are not O.K. with it," said Nikita Likhachev, editor in chief of TJournal, an online publication covering internet culture, technology and politics.

With no public accountability, nobody has any real sense of the scope of the shutdown, he said. "The whole point about the internet being broken in Russia is that we don't know what is happening and whether it can be fixed at all," Mr. Likhachev said.

Countless people who play online games or use specialized services and tend to be apolitical, Mr. Likhachev said, have suddenly realized how much the government can affect their daily lives. "They have started asking questions about what is happening," he said.

At the rally, which was peaceful, one hand-painted sign reflected that mood: "Things are so bad that even introverts are here."

No arrests were reported.

The rally, organized by Russia's small Libertarian Party, had an official permit — often a sign that the government knows that a broad segment of the population is angry. The roster of speakers included opposition stalwarts like Aleksei A. Navalny, the anticorruption activist. He led chants of "Down with the Czar!" and called on people to continue to fight censorship at the May 5 rally he has called nationwide to protest Mr. Putin's inauguration for a fourth term.

Various speakers and demonstrators said they had never been to any public demonstration before.

Alexander Gornik, 34, a software entrepreneur, said many of the tools that his employees use for work, like Slack, Pipedrive and Tralier, were now inaccessible. To make high-quality software that can compete globally, Russia needs to be connected to the world, he said.

"This is not just about Telegram, it is an attempt to isolate the Russian segment of the internet," Mr. Gornik said.

Despite all the attention paid to Russian hacking and other expertise on the internet, the programmers at the government regulatory agency have not been capable of handling the complicated process of shutting down an app with international reach.

Mr. Durov, who left Russia after his previous creation, Vkontakte, was wrestled away from him in 2014, generated countless additional I.P. addresses to thwart efforts to block Telegram. Some 13 million Russians are among its 200 million users worldwide, and many in Russia can still access the site. Mr. Durov encouraged the demonstrators from afar with a series of posts on Vkontakte.

"Russia is at a crossroads — full-scale censorship has not yet been introduced," he wrote in one post. "If action is not taken, Russia will lose Telegram and other popular services."

Under sunny skies in the early afternoon, he posted again, writing: "Thousands of young and progressive people are at this moment speaking out in Moscow in defense of the internet. This is unprecedented."

In recent months, the Putin administration, particularly the Foreign Ministry, has repeatedly accused the West of "Russophobia" for sanctions and the general sour mood toward Russia.

One rally organizer turned that accusation on its head, telling the demonstrators that it was various politicians and bureaucrats who were shutting down the internet who were really afraid of the Russian people. He began shouting the names of some of them followed by "Russophobe," and the entire crowd chanted with him.

There was no immediate government reaction to the protest.

Many of the demonstrators carried paper airplanes, the symbol of Telegram, which whipped around above the heads of the crowd.

The turnout of many thousands was particularly notable in that Monday was the start of a weeklong holiday, when Muscovites depart the city in droves for the country or abroad. A second rally is planned for Tuesday in St. Petersburg.

Polina Oleinik, 17, and Polina Bulakh, 16, both students, said it was the first demonstration that they had ever attended.

"Young people between the ages of 15 and 30 are very upset about this," Ms. Oleinik said. "Russia must be a democratic country free of censorship. That is why we came."

SOPHIA KISHKOVSKY contributed reporting.

Russia, Accused of Faking News, Unfurls Its Own 'Fake News' Bill

BY LINCOLN PIGMAN | JULY 22, 2018

MOSCOW — Russia, which American intelligence agencies said spread its fair share of misinformation during the 2016 United States election, says it will crack down on "fake news" at home, with a proposed law that critics say could limit freedom of speech on the internet.

The bill, submitted by lawmakers from the governing party, United Russia, proposes holding social networks accountable for "inaccurate" comments users post. Under existing Russian law, social media users can be punished for content deemed to promote homosexuality, to threaten public order or to be "extremist" in nature, with fines as well as prison time.

Under the proposed rule, part of a creeping crackdown on digital rights under President Vladimir V. Putin, websites with more than 100,000 daily visitors and a commenting feature must take down factually inaccurate posts or face a fine of up to 50 million rubles, about $800,000.

The bill gives social media companies 24 hours to delete "inaccurate" information after being notified of its existence, raising concerns that moderators will be left to interpret the term, which is vaguely defined in the measure.

The legislation has passed one of three votes in Parliament.

Critics worry that out of an abundance of caution, moderators are likely to interpret truthfulness to the authorities' advantage. They say the bill would make it easier for the state to pressure social media companies to cooperate with security services by requiring them to establish offices in Russia, a step that the social media giants Facebook and Twitter have avoided so as not to fall under Russian legal jurisdiction.

Internet companies, which have often borne the financial costs of restrictions in Russia, say that too many people write posts and leave comments for moderators to thoroughly review every potential instance of false news within 24 hours.

The bill "will become an instrument of censorship" unless social media companies develop algorithms to distinguish real news from fake news, removing the human element and potential bias, Vladimir V. Zykov, the head of an association of social media users in Russia, warned in a recent meeting with lawmakers.

Human rights advocates say the bill holds clear echoes of the term frequently used by President Trump. Adrian Shahbaz, a research manager at Freedom House, said Mr. Trump's "use of 'fake news' as a catchall term for media outlets he does not like" has inspired crackdowns on press freedom around the world.

"As with the term 'terrorist,' it has basically become an insult used to smear and discredit opponents," he added.

Still, "the proliferation of deliberately falsified information online is a widely recognized problem," even as efforts to counter it can be abused, Mr. Shahbaz said. Already this year, at least five countries have passed laws regulating fake news online, he added.

These governments have taken different approaches. In May, Kenya banned information that is "calculated or results in panic, chaos or violence," or that is "likely to discredit the reputation of a person." Malaysia, like Russia, chose a different tact, targeting false information regardless of its consequences. In April, Malaysia's lower house of Parliament passed a bill outlawing fake news, the first measure of its kind in the world. France is weighing its own measure.

Russian lawmakers have also noticed these initiatives — some meant to counter Russian-made fake news — and have co-opted their language and arguments. Marina A. Mukabenova, deputy chairwoman of a Parliament committee on information policy, told the daily newspaper Nezavisimaya Gazeta that fake news sparked "heated discussion" and divided Russian society.

In contrast with debates on fake news in the United States and Europe, Russian lawmakers seem most focused on domestic dissent, rather than foreign meddling. For example, the bill's co-sponsor, Sergei M. Boyarsky, pointed to what he suggested was a clear-cut case of damaging online information: a flurry of posts that exaggerated the death toll of a mall fire in Siberia.

"The tragedy in Kemerovo showed how vulnerable our information space within social networks is to the falsification of information," he told the news agency Tass.

And yet, in the fire's aftermath, relatives of victims accused the authorities of hiding the true death toll, writing social media posts that helped spur protests and calls for local officials to resign. True or not, the fatality figures posted online became central to a national debate in one of the first domestic crises of Mr. Putin's fourth presidential term. The proposed law, though, would have squelched this debate.

Activists are skeptical that the authorities have Russians' best interests at heart. The language of public safety often conceals efforts at censorship, said Artem Kozlyuk, the founder of Roskomsvoboda, an anti-censorship website. The end result, he said, is always "expansion of the government's powers and censorship."

In Russia, a Top University Lacks Just One Thing: Students

BY IVAN NECHEPURENKO | AUG. 26, 2018

ST. PETERSBURG, RUSSIA — At this time of year, the halls of the European University at St. Petersburg, a private liberal arts college in the heart of Russia's second-largest city, would normally be filling with students returning from summer break.

For the second year in a row, however, the college's lecture halls are empty and dark, and the canteen is filled with an eerie silence. The only signs of life are in the faculty rooms, where the underemployed professors grumble about their enforced sabbatical.

The European University has a world-class faculty, a generous endowment and an outstanding reputation as a research institution. What it has lacked since August of last year, when the authorities took away the university's teaching license, is students.

When that happened, the students were forced to leave and the university began a desperate search for high-ranking backers in the Russian government. At times, that seemed like a lost cause, even after President Vladimir V. Putin signed three resolutions ordering officials to support the school.

Lately, however, things have begun to look up. Mr. Putin's re-election in March led to a major reshuffle of the Russian government. Aleksei L. Kudrin, a longtime associate of Mr. Putin and one of the most powerful liberal-leaning politicians in Russia, became the head of the Audit Chamber, with the power to send his own inspectors.

Suddenly, with Mr. Kudrin's appointment, the Russian education regulator failed to find any violations when it surveyed the university, and a teaching license was granted this month. It now plans to reopen to students in October.

But the European University's struggles may not be over. There have been times over the past year when the school thought its teaching

Roman V. Popov, left, a student of economics, with Kirill Y. Borissov, a professor of economics. Mr. Popov had to transfer to another college to receive his degree.

license was about to be restored, and each time its hopes were dashed. The university was caught in the seesaw battles waged in the Russian government between reactionary, nationalist forces and more progressive, outward-looking factions.

It is not just the European University that the nationalists have in their sights. Last month, the Russian government revoked the accreditation of the Moscow School of Social and Economic Sciences, another highly regarded Western-oriented institution.

The attacks underscore questions about how Russia can build independent, world-class institutions if they are constantly pressured by revanchist elements in the Russian leadership.

"The European University's problem is that it is European," said Vladimir Y. Gelman, one of Russia's leading political scientists, who is a professor at the school. "The set of principles followed by our school — academic freedom, self-organization, and international openness — is the opposite of the one followed by today's Russia: centralized control, power vertical and isolationism," he said. "We are not compatible with these principles."

The European University was a product of the immediate post-Soviet era, when money was scarce but grass-roots initiatives blossomed. It was set up in 1994 by a group of enthusiasts to try to prevent brain drain. Its aim was to bring together Russia's leading scholars in the social sciences and humanities in an institution modeled after Western universities.

In those early years, it enjoyed generous funding from Western donors such as George Soros's Open Society Foundations and the Ford and MacArthur Foundations. Later on, as those groups fell from favor, wealthy Russian industrialists pitched in.

The school was a success almost from the day it opened its doors, with students flocking there from all over Russia and from around the world. In contrast to most Russian universities, students were forced to think critically, and they were free to choose their own areas of interest.

The Soviet educational system had produced good mathematicians and physicists, but little else, with the disciplines of economics, sociology, political science and history burdened by Marxist dogma.

"Soviet economics was simply a collection of ideological symbols and scholastic constructions." said Kirill Y. Borissov, a professor of economics at the European University. "Even the teachings of Marx and Lenin were misinterpreted. It had nothing to do with economics as such."

To bring leading teaching and research practices to Russia, the university hired Russian academics who had left for leading schools in the West, including Oxford, Cambridge and several leading American universities.

"The European University is probably the best thing that can happen to a scholar of humanities or social sciences in Russia," said another professor there, Ivan I. Kurilla, a leading specialist on Russian-American relations. "Most Russian academics dream to work like this. We spend our time writing, researching and teaching, instead of fighting the endless bureaucracy."

MAXIM BABENKO FOR THE NEW YORK TIMES

Ivan I. Kurilla.

The university invited guest lecturers and permanent professors from outside Russia. In 2016, the Russian Education Ministry named the school the top research university in the country, above the famed Moscow State University. One of the reasons for this success was the absence of censorship, said Grigorii V. Golosov, one of the most-cited Russian political scientists.

"For instance, today you cannot be part of the international scientific community if you don't recognize that the Russian political regime is authoritarian," he said. "For the vast majority of scientists, this is just an accepted fact."

But not for Russia's nationalists, whose influence grew steadily in the years after Mr. Putin's rise to the presidency in 2000. Soon, they were making trouble for the university, which they saw as an intolerable outpost of Western liberalism.

The revocation of its teaching license was only one of several attacks on the university over the past decade. Fire inspectors banned classes for six weeks in 2008, apparently after the college accepted a grant from the European Commission for a program to improve election monitoring in Russia. After the university returned the grant, the fire inspectors dropped their complaints.

In 2016, Vitaly V. Milonov, an ultraconservative legislator best known for his anti-gay activities, filed a complaint with the Office of the Prosecutor General saying that his constituents were concerned about what was being taught at the school. Two other complaints were filed within the next three months.

One of those, Vyacheslav Y. Dobrokhotov, an activist with a nationalist movement in St. Petersburg, cited a book by Oleg V. Kharkhordin, a political scientist at the university, which argued that the Soviet social fabric was largely based on hypocrisy.

"I realized that this organization is harmful to Russia," Mr. Dobrokhotov said of the school. "Its main organizer is the United States. They want to stage a color revolution in our country."

The other grievance was filed by Dmitri Bikbov, who complained about illegal migrant workers unloading new plastic windows near the university's main building, an 18th-century, marble-clad palace that had been designated a historical landmark. In an interview, Mr. Bikbov said that he had nothing against the university and that he had been asked to make a complaint by a government official he did not want to identify.

The complaints created a legal pretext for no fewer than 11 official bodies — among them the education watchdog, which issues the teaching licenses; the St. Petersburg government, which owns the palace building; and the Emergency Situations Ministry, which oversees fire inspection — to conduct inquiries. A legal wrangle ensued.

In the end, the St. Petersburg government evicted the university from the palace — because of the plastic windows, which were only temporary — forcing it to move to an ordinary building across the street.

University officials say they were never clear why the teaching

MAXIM BABENKO FOR THE NEW YORK TIMES

Dmitri Bikbov said he had been asked to make a complaint against the university by a government official he did not want to identify.

license was revoked. They say the authorities cited the failure of the university's political scientists to work outside the campus, and its lack of a proper gym.

"I am sure the reason we cannot study has nothing to do with fire safety regulations," said Roman V. Popov, a student of economics, who had to transfer to another college in St. Petersburg to receive his degree. "It might be political, or perhaps someone just wanted to have our building."

While the university may now be back on its feet, some faculty members said they were disappointed with what they described as the administration's subservient stance over the past year.

"The ability to make a deal with the government was good, but at one point, it turned into a catastrophe," said Yevgeny V. Anisimov, one of the leading historians in Russia. "We lost students, we lost our building. The one we have now is still empty."

Ai Weiwei: How Censorship Works

OPINION | BY AI WEIWEI | MAY 6, 2017

BEIJING — In the space of a month in 2014, at separate art exhibitions in Beijing and Shanghai that included my work, my name was blotted out — in one case by government officials and by exhibitors themselves in the other case. Some people might take such treatment in stride, as nothing to get huffy about. But as an artist, I view the labels on my work as a measure of the value I have produced — like water-level markers at a riverbank. Other people might just shrug, but I can't. I have no illusions, though, that my unwillingness to shrug affects anyone else's willingness to do so.

Life in China is saturated with pretense. People feign ignorance and speak in ambiguities. Everyone in China knows that a censorship system exists, but there is very little discussion of why it exists.

At first glance, the censorship seems invisible, but its omnipresent washing of people's feelings and perceptions creates limits on the information people receive, select and rely upon. The content offered by the Chinese state media, after its processing by political censors, is not free information. It is information that has been chosen, filtered and assigned its place, inevitably restricting the free and independent will of readers and viewers.

The harm of a censorship system is not just that it impoverishes intellectual life; it also fundamentally distorts the rational order in which the natural and spiritual worlds are understood. The censorship system relies on robbing a person of the self-perception that one needs in order to maintain an independent existence. It cuts off one's access to independence and happiness.

Censoring speech removes the freedom to choose what to take in and to express to others, and this inevitably leads to depression in people. Wherever fear dominates, true happiness vanishes and individual willpower runs dry. Judgments become distorted and rationality

JON HAN

itself begins to slip away. Group behavior can become wild, abnormal and violent.

Whenever the state controls or blocks information, it not only reasserts its absolute power; it also elicits from the people whom it rules a voluntary submission to the system and an acknowledgment of its dominion. This, in turn, supports the axiom of the debased: Accept dependency in return for practical benefits.

The most elegant way to adjust to censorship is to engage in self-censorship. It is the perfect method for allying with power and setting the stage for the mutual exchange of benefit. The act of kowtowing to power in order to receive small pleasures may seem minor; but without it, the brutal assault of the censorship system would not be possible.

For people who accept this passive position toward authority, "getting by" becomes the supreme value. They smile, bow and nod their heads, and such behavior usually leads to lifestyles that are comfortable, trouble free and even cushy. This attitude is essentially defensive on their part. It is obvious that in any dispute, if one side is silenced, the words of the other side will go unquestioned.

That's what we have here in China: The self-silenced majority, sycophants of a powerful regime, resentful of people like me who speak out, are doubly bitter because they know that their debasement comes by their own hand. Thus self-defense also becomes self-comfort.

Because the censorship system needs cooperation and tacit understanding from the censored, I disagree with the common view that the censored are simply its victims. Voluntary self-censorship brings benefits to a person, and the system would not work if the voluntary aspect were not there.

People who willingly censor themselves are vulnerable to moral challenges of many kinds. They have never been victims and never will be, despite their occasional show of tear wiping. Each time they display their servility, they bring warmth to the hearts of the authoritarians and harm to people who protest. Their craven stance, as it becomes widespread, also becomes the deeper reason for the moral collapse of our society. If these people believe that their choice to cooperate is the only way to avoid victimhood, they are embarking on an ill-fated journey in the dark.

The system rewards ordinary people for their cooperation automatically; there is no need for them to compete for the rewards. Managers of artistic and cultural projects, though, need to do more than that; they need to show proactively that they "get it" and will accommodate the authoritarians and protect their public image. They know that if anything causes unhappiness higher up, a project, and perhaps an organization, will be scrubbed.

In this kind of system, where works of art rise or fall not in free competition but by corrupt criteria, any creator of art that has any genuine vitality must act dumb and agree to tacit understandings.

It is well known that I cannot speak in any public forum. My name is expunged everywhere in the public media. I am not allowed to travel within China and am banned from the state media, where I am regularly scolded. Commentators in the state media pretend to be even-handed, but that's impossible, given where they sit, behind the state's protective curtain. They don't address topics like the right to free speech or the quality of life for the vast majority of Chinese. Their special expertise is in unscrupulous attacks on voices that have already been repressed.

My *virtual* existence, if we can call it that, exists only among people who notice me by choice, and those people fall clearly into two categories: those who see my behavior as strengthening the meaning of their lives and those who see me as obstructing their roads to benefit, and for that reason cannot pardon me.

Only when China offers fair and just platforms for expression of public opinion will we have ways of meeting minds by using our words. I support the establishment of such platforms. This should be the first principle in making social justice possible. But in a place where everything is fake, right down to the last hair, anyone who stands up to quibble about truth seems naïve, even childlike. In the end, I find the "naïve" route the only one left open to me. I am obliged to be as narrow-minded as those "narrow-minded" Uighurs and Tibetans we hear about.

An artist is a mover, a political participant. Especially in times of historic change, aesthetic values will always have an advantage. A society that persecutes people who persist in cleaving to individual values is an uncivilized society that has no future.

When a person's values are put on public display, the standards and ethics of that person and of the society as a whole may be challenged. An individual's free expression can stimulate a more distinctive kind of exchange and will, in turn, lead to more distinctive ways of exchanging views. This principle is inherent in my philosophy of art.

The censorship in China places limits on knowledge and values, which is the key to imposing ideological slavery. I do what I can to show cruelties, the subtle and the not so subtle. As things are here today, rational resistance can be based only on the small actions of individual people. Where I fail, the responsibility is mine alone, but the rights I seek to defend are ones that can be shared.

Ideological slaves, too, can revolt. In the end, they always do.

AI WEIWEI is an artist. This article is adapted from an essay in the forthcoming "Rules for Resistance: Advice From Around the Globe for the Age of Trump." It was translated by Perry Link from the Chinese.

After Criticism, Publisher Reverses Decision to Bow to China's Censors

BY CHRIS BUCKLEY | AUG. 21, 2017

BEIJING — One of the world's leading academic publishers, Cambridge University Press, on Monday abruptly reversed its decision to bow to censorship of a leading journal on contemporary China, after its agreement to remove offending papers from its website in China ignited condemnation from academics.

The Cambridge University Press said last week that it had gone along with the demands from a Chinese publishing import agency and cut 315 papers from the online version of the journal, The China Quarterly, that can be read in China.

Academics criticized the decision as a worrisome intrusion of censorship into international academic research, where the Chinese government has become increasingly energetic in pushing its views, and in discouraging work that offends it.

The pressure from academics worked.

Tim Pringle, the editor of The China Quarterly, said on Twitter that the press "intends to repost immediately the articles removed from its website in China." Professor Pringle said the decision was made "after a justifiably intense reaction from the global academic community and beyond."

Professor Pringle said in a telephone interview from London that Cambridge University Press would also make the reposted papers available free of charge, doing away with the hefty charge that one-time readers of the site usually pay.

"It puts academic freedom where it needs to be, which is ahead of economic concerns," Professor Pringle said.

Cambridge University Press said in an online statement that its decision to cut the papers had been temporary, ahead of planned talks with the publishing agent that have not yet been held. "The university's academic leadership and the press have agreed to reinstate the blocked content, with immediate effect, so as to uphold the principle of academic freedom on which the university's work is founded," it said.

On Tuesday, searches for potentially sensitive topics like "Tiananmen" on the Cambridge University Press's webpage for The China Quarterly indicated that many papers and reviews were now downloadable free of charge, including in China.

Now, though, the Press may have to prepare itself for potential repercussions from the Chinese censors, who are unlikely to be happy with the public rebuke and reversal. It was unclear how the 315 academic articles that they said offended official sensibilities would now be censored, if at all.

"If China perceives the reversal as a matter of face or a challenge or whatever, I imagine it will escalate upward and Cambridge University Press will face further issues with China," said Jonathan Sullivan, a China studies scholar at the University of Nottingham who is on The China Quarterly's executive committee.

The China Quarterly has long been one of the world's most prestigious venues for research on modern China. Increasingly it has published work by scholars in or originally from China. The latest issue of the journal includes papers on ideological currents in journalism education and on political tension in Hong Kong.

But a Chinese agency that manages imported publications told the Press to cut papers and book reviews on subjects including Hong Kong, Tibet, Xinjiang, the Cultural Revolution and the 1989 crackdown on student-led protests based in Tiananmen Square.

At first, Cambridge University Press went along. "We complied with this initial request to remove individual articles, to ensure that other academic and educational materials we publish remain available to researchers and educators in this market," the Press said last week in a statement.

Several academics denounced the decision, and one started a petition that called for a boycott of the publisher if it did not reverse its decision.

"It is disturbing to academics and universities worldwide that China is attempting to export its censorship on topics that do not fit its preferred narrative," said the petition, started by Christopher Balding, an associate professor at the Peking University HSBC Business School in the southern Chinese city of Shenzhen.

Professor Balding said in an interview on Monday that he welcomed the latest decision by Cambridge University Press, but that research and publishing still risked buckling to political or economic pressure from China.

"Hopefully, this will prompt greater thinking about how to effectively engage with China," Professor Balding said. "Continued acquiescence is not the answer."

China's Oppression Reaches Beyond Its Borders

OPINION | BY LAUREN HILGERS | APRIL 9, 2018

Ms. Hilgers lived in Shanghai for six years. She is the author of "Patriot Number One: American Dreams in Chinatown," from which this essay is adapted.

THE FIRST THREATENING phone call that Zhuang Liehong got in New York was in the fall of 2016, on a gloriously warm September morning. The call came from a jail where his father was being held following a protest in Mr. Zhuang's home village in Southern China. "Is this Zhuang Liehong?" asked an unfamiliar voice. When Mr. Zhuang said yes, there was a pause and his father's voice came on the line. "Son," he said, "stop doing what you're doing. It will be bad for your family."

What Mr. Zhuang had been doing, for the most part, was posting on Facebook. He was putting up photos that had been sent by friends and family, which recorded a police crackdown that had swept his home village, Wukan. Five years earlier, during the fall of 2011, Mr. Zhuang had been a ringleader in a series of protests that overtook the little seaside village. He had helped alert his fellow villagers to land grabs that were chipping away at village boundaries and filling the pockets of local officials. When those protests ended, it seemed the villagers had emerged victorious. Villagers had been granted the right to hold local elections, and Mr. Zhuang was one of seven new village committee members tasked with administrating the village and returning stolen land.

Back then, Wukan was held up among democracy activists as a symbol of liberalization, a hopeful sign that China was open to political change. But the elections were misleading, the hope misplaced. Mr. Zhuang fled to New York in 2014. Two years later, he found himself answering that phone call in New York City, swept up in new political currents. The Communist Party of China was taking a recent crackdown on dissent and moving it over borders. Mr. Zhuang had moved to the United States to speak freely about his village. In his father's voice he heard the ventriloquism of the corrupt officials who had sold off his village land. Mr. Zhuang guessed that his father was surrounded by security personnel. He felt the phone call suggested a trade — his father's freedom for Mr. Zhuang's silence.

Since 2015, a sweeping crackdown on internal dissent has ensnared hundreds of human rights lawyers, feminists, journalists and democracy activists. China now spends more on internal security than it does on its military. And as the crackdown continues at home, the Chinese Communist Party has started to expand its reach, looking to enforce censorship, increase surveillance and silence dissent across borders. Their targets have included academics, exiled business elites, former judges and activists like Mr. Zhuang.

In a twist, as states across the globe retrench and solidify their hold, the quest for centralized rule and the quashing of dissent have caused borders to become porous. Russia stands accused of poisoning a former spy living in Britain. Turkish thugs attacked a crowd of protesters in Washington, D.C., during a visit by Turkey's authoritarian-leaning president, Recep Tayyip Erdogan. Some of these tactics are old. Autocratic regimes have long sought to eliminate former spies living abroad. Detaining family members as a proxy for a high-profile dissident in exile is an old practice. Technology, however, has decreased the price of harassment. The same tools that enabled the uprisings in the Arab Spring, the same ones that help Mr. Zhuang promote his cause, make surveillance and intimidation easier. Now anonymous teenagers can harass on Twitter and so can agents of state.

The warning call that Mr. Zhuang got from his father would not be the last. Over the next few months, they kept coming. Mr. Zhuang had several phones, and if he stopped answering one, the calls would appear on another. Security officers tracked the phones of his friends and interrogated them if they accepted calls from Mr. Zhuang. A CCTV camera mysteriously appeared outside the door of the home that Mr.

SUSANNA GENTILI

Zhuang's mother shared with his handicapped older brother. Friends and family no longer visited. His father was sentenced to three years in prison and kept sending warnings. His mother called him from her ramshackle home in Wukan. When she called, she warned her son that, even in the United States, he was not safe.

The extended reach of the Chinese government has affected exiles and immigrants across the world. In Canada, a former Supreme People's Court judge, Xie Wendong, reported that his sister and son had both been detained by security forces. Chinese government agents sent a lawyer to Canada to try to persuade him to return to China. Authorities also ordered Xie's ex-wife to bring him back to China, threatening her with detention if she failed. In France, Zheng Ning, a former businessman, was successfully pursued by Chinese agents and ended up returning to China. In a report released in January, the Citizen Lab, a research group based at the University of Toronto, recorded a phishing operation that ran for 19 months, targeting Tibetans, the Falun Gong-related publication The Epoch Times and groups of ethnic Uyghurs.

In the United States, scholars studying China have also reported that phishing scams and targeted malware have become a matter of routine — with repeated attempts to access research and identify sources. An outspoken Chinese student at the University of Georgia recently told Radio Free Asia that he had received a call from a Chinese security officer, asking him to inform on other Chinese students and activists. Ethnic Uyghur journalists now living in the United States have reported the disappearance of multiple family members still in China.

Chen Xiaoping, a journalist at the Long Island-based, Mandarin-language media company Mirror Media Group, issued an open letter on Twitter in January asking the Chinese government to release his wife, who had been missing in China for 90 days. She had disappeared shortly after Mr. Chen began interviewing the exiled Chinese billionaire Guo Wengui. Soon after Mr. Chen released the letter, a video was anonymously posted on YouTube — a tape of his wife denouncing his work in the United States.

The threats that Mr. Zhuang has received have not dissuaded him from continuing to protest China's government. They have, however, stolen his peace of mind. The political problems that Mr. Zhuang had were, he felt, with the local government in Guangdong Province. He assumed those officials would not be able to reach him in New York. And then, when the phone calls started coming, he began to doubt himself.

Mr. Zhuang, like so many other exiled Chinese citizens, is finding that he is still subject to Beijing's demands. Worldwide, China's government is sending a chilling message: no matter where you are, speaking freely comes at a steep price.

LAUREN HILGERS is a journalist and the author of "Patriot Number One: American Dreams in Chinatown."

Twitter Users in China Face Detention and Threats in New Beijing Crackdown

BY PAUL MOZUR | JAN. 10, 2019

SHANGHAI — One man spent 15 days in a detention center. The police threatened another's family. A third was chained to a chair for eight hours of interrogation.

Their offense: posting on Twitter.

The Chinese police, in a sharp escalation of the country's online censorship efforts, are questioning and detaining a growing number of Twitter users even though the social media platform is blocked in China and the vast majority of people in the country cannot see it.

The crackdown is the latest front in President Xi Jinping's campaign to suppress internet activity. In effect, the authorities are extending their control over Chinese citizens' online lives, even if what they post is unlikely to be seen in the country.

"If we give up Twitter, we are losing one of our last places to speak," said Wang Aizhong, a human-rights activist who said the police had told him to delete messages criticizing the Chinese government.

When Beijing is unable to get activists to delete tweets, others will sometimes do the job. Mr. Wang refused to take down his tweets. Then, one night last month while he was reading a book, his phone buzzed with text messages from Twitter that contained backup codes to his account.

An hour later, he said, 3,000 of his tweets had been deleted. He blamed government-affiliated hackers, although those who were responsible and the methods they used could not be independently confirmed.

A Twitter spokeswoman declined to comment on the government campaign.

China has long policed what its citizens can see and say, including online, but the recent push shows that Beijing's vision of internet control encompasses social media around the world. Messages on WhatsApp, which is blocked in China, have begun to appear as evidence in Chinese trials.

The Chinese government has increasingly demanded that Google and Facebook take down content that officials object to even though both companies' sites are inaccessible in China. After the exiled Chinese billionaire Guo Wengui used the platforms to lob graft accusations at top Chinese leaders, Facebook and Twitter suspended his accounts temporarily, citing user complaints and the disclosure of personal information.

Twitter may be banned in China, but the platform plays an important role in political debate and the discussion of issues in the country. To access the service, a small but active community uses software to circumvent the government's controls over what people can see online. According to an estimate based on a survey of 1,627 Chinese internet users last year by Daniela Stockmann, a professor at the Hertie School of Governance in Germany, only 0.4 percent of China's internet users, roughly 3.2 million people, use Twitter.

While it remains off limits for people in China, official media outlets like the Communist Party-controlled People's Daily newspaper and the Xinhua news agency have used Twitter to shape perceptions of the country in the rest of the world.

"On the one hand, state media takes advantage of the full features of these platforms to reach millions of people," said Sarah Cook, a senior analyst for East Asia at Freedom House, a pro-democracy research group based in the United States. "On the other hand, ordinary Chinese are risking interrogation and jail for using these same platforms to communicate with each other and the outside world."

LinkedIn, the business networking service and one of the few American social media outlets allowed in China, has long bowed to the country's censors. It briefly took down the Chinese accounts of Peter Humphrey, a British private investigator who was once imprisoned in China, last month and Zhou Fengsuo, a human-rights activist, this month. The company sent emails to both containing language similar to the messages it sends users when it removes posts that violate censorship rules.

"What we've seen in recent weeks is the authorities desperately escalating the censorship of social media," Mr. Humphrey said. "I think it's quite astonishing that on this cloak-and-dagger basis, LinkedIn has been gagging people and preventing their comments from being seen in China."

Both accounts have been restored. In a statement, LinkedIn apologized for taking the accounts down and said it had done so by accident. "Our Trust and Safety team is updating our internal processes to help prevent an error like this from happening again," the statement said.

With Twitter, Chinese officials are targeting a vibrant platform for Chinese activists.

Interviews with nine Twitter users questioned by the police and a review of a recording of a four-hour interrogation found a similar pattern: The police would produce printouts of tweets and advise users to delete either the specific messages or their entire accounts. Officers would often complain about posts that were critical of the Chinese government or that specifically mentioned Mr. Xi.

The police have used threats and, sometimes, physical restraints, according to Twitter users who were questioned. Huang Chengcheng, an activist with more than 8,000 Twitter followers, said his hands and feet were manacled to a chair while he was interrogated for eight hours in Chongqing. When the inquiry was over, he signed a promise to stay off Twitter.

Those pulled in for questioning do not necessarily have the biggest presence on the social network. Pan Xidian, a 47-year-old construction company employee in Xiamen with about 4,000 followers, posted a comic by a dissident cartoonist known as Rebel Pepper, along with criticism of human-rights crackdowns. In November, the police called him in for 20 hours of questioning. After being forced to delete several tweets, he was allowed to go, and he thought his ordeal was over.

But officers showed up at his workplace a short time later and threw him into a car. They asked him to sign a document that said he had disturbed the social order. He complied. Then they showed him a second document, which said he would be detained. He spent the next two weeks in a cell with 10 other people, watching propaganda videos.

"In this era, we certainly know fear, but I can't control myself," Mr. Pan said while crying during a phone interview after he was released. "We've been living a very suppressed life."

"We're like lambs," he added. "They're taking us one after another. We have no ability to fight back."

The crackdown is unusually broad and punitive. When censoring domestic social media in the past, officials have targeted prominent users. People were questioned or detained less frequently and more haphazardly.

The current push appears to be well coordinated between local and national law enforcement authorities, said Xiao Qiang, a professor at the School of Information at the University of California, Berkeley.

"Actually taking nationwide action, physically calling in all of these people, we've never seen that before," he said.

The new approach involves broad action by China's powerful Ministry of Public Security, which oversees law enforcement and political security. Several Twitter users said local authorities had specifically cited the internet police, a branch of the security ministry that monitors online activity. The agency, which refers to such local enforcement as "touching the ground," was taken over last summer by a hard-liner known for a crackdown on telecom fraud in Xiamen, a city on the southeast coast.

The security ministry and the Cyberspace Administration of China, which regulates the internet, did not respond to faxed requests for comment.

The police have impressed upon activists that they can see posts outside China's wall of censorship. After a four-hour grilling of a Twitter user with a small following who had complained in a post about the environment, a police officer offered him some advice. The user, who spoke on the condition of anonymity for fear of further reprisal, recorded the interrogation and provided a copy of the audio.

"Delete all your tweets, and shut down your account," the officer said. "Everything on the internet can be monitored, even the inappropriate comments in WeChat groups," a reference to a popular Chinese messaging app.

"This is truly wholehearted advice for you," the officer added. "If this happens a second time, it will be handled differently. It will affect your parents. You are still so young. If you get married and have kids, it will affect them."

The efforts have dampened debate on Chinese-language Twitter, said Yaqiu Wang, a China researcher with Human Rights Watch, who chronicled the crackdown in November. Still, not all users have gone quietly.

"Many activists want free speech," Ms. Wang said in an interview. "Even when they're harassed and intimidated, they're very brave and continue to tweet. This is an act of defiance to censorship and oppression."

LI YUAN contributed reporting from Hong Kong. QIQING LIN contributed research.

Netflix's Bow to Saudi Censors Comes at a Cost to Free Speech

COLUMN | BY JIM RUTENBERG | JAN. 6, 2019

UNDER ARTICLE 6, Paragraph 1 of Saudi Arabia's Anti-Cyber Crime Law, the following is punishable by up to five years in prison: "Production, preparation, transmission, or storage of material impinging on public order, religious values, public morals, and privacy, through the information network or computers."

Think "First Amendment." Then invert it.

Last week, we learned that the Kingdom had alerted Netflix that it had violated the statute with an episode of its comedy show "Patriot Act," starring Hasan Minhaj, a comedian and American Muslim. How? Mr. Minhaj dared to question Crown Prince Mohammed bin Salman, both for the C.I.A.'s conclusion he ordered the murder of the Saudi dissident Jamal Khashoggi and for Saudi war atrocities in Yemen.

Maybe the Saudi complaint wasn't all that shocking. Like any authoritarian monarch worth his bone saw, Prince Mohammed doesn't brook criticism, which is why he has overseen the Saudis' increased jailing of journalists, critics and rivals.

The shock came with Netflix's supine compliance. After pulling the episode from its Saudi feed, the streaming service told The Financial Times it was simply responding to "a valid legal request."

Add another 10 paces to America's retreat from its place at the forefront of free speech and political expression.

It was but one episode in one country. And Saudis who were burning to see it could still find it on YouTube.

But each small step for dictatorial crackdowns abetted by American leaders — be they in politics or business — is one giant leap for the forces that are now so successfully stanching free expression and dissent across the world.

L'affaire Netflix raises a big question: As America's new media overlords grow at a stunning rate, expanding into every nook and cranny of the globe where governments will let them in, are they compelled to defend universal values like free speech that their home country was founded on?

Increasingly, it seems, profit, expansion and perhaps a wee bit of cowardice are trumping the very principles that made the United States entertainment and news industries what they are — and that made a Netflix possible in the first place.

I'm not so naïve that I don't understand that this is the cost of becoming a dominant media player now, when success is measured by how many more hundreds of millions of users a company can attract.

"Stock price is measuring expected future earnings and those turn on global user numbers," said Sam Blatteis, the former public policy lead for Google and YouTube in the Gulf and now chief executive for MENA Catalysts, a Middle East government affairs consulting firm.

Growth lies in emerging markets, many of which may be run by less-than-savory characters ruling by less-than-savory means.

"Companies have to walk this tightrope between their cosmopolitan values on one side and realizing that going abroad into many emerging markets is a contact sport," Mr. Blatteis, speaking from Dubai, told me last week. "You have to roll up your sleeves and that can involve adapting and compromise."

That's why Apple acquiesced to China's demand that it remove various apps that bypassed the country's censors as well as the news apps of The New York Times.

It's why Hollywood pulled back from making films critical of China (getting a bounty of Chinese movie financing in return).

At the risk of hurting Mark Zuckerberg's feelings, it's why Facebook has agreed to demands from countries like Turkey, the United Arab Emirates and Pakistan to restrict access to posts deemed illegal because they criticized those countries' leaders or founders.

And it's why, after Prince Mohammed said he would end a 35-year ban on movie theaters in the kingdom, entertainment moguls including Ari Emanuel, Robert A. Iger, and Mr. Murdoch feted him last spring at intimate dinners around Los Angeles, despite news of repression in the kingdom and civilian deaths in Yemen.

Then came the killing of Mr. Khashoggi, who wrote columns for The Washington Post that were critical of the crown prince. According to United States intelligence, Prince Mohammed had ordered Mr. Khashoggi's death, which his men carried out with slasher-flick aplomb, reportedly using a bone saw to dismember his body.

That wasn't enough for President Trump, who sowed doubt about the intelligence conclusion while praising Saudi Arabia for "keeping oil prices at reasonable levels." The message on human rights and the First Amendment: Make me an offer.

Mr. Trump didn't invent realpolitik. But previously, even when American actions contradicted its vision of itself, presidential paeans to democratic norms carried at least symbolic weight.

Netflix had an opportunity to send a different message.

"Even more because Trump and the White House have been so much putting money over lives, frankly, I'd hoped that this was where American businesses could take a stand," said The Post's global opinions editor Karen Attiah, who edited Mr. Khashoggi's columns. "Netflix really had a chance to stand up for values and for Hasan."

At the very least, she said, Netflix should have never called the Saudis' legal request "valid," even if it believed it had to comply to maintain its presence in the country.

Netflix wouldn't answer my question about what made the request "valid." In a statement to me, its general counsel, David Hyman, said, "Our programs push the boundaries on important social and other issues in many places around the world." But, he added, "to run a global service" the company has to abide by foreign laws "even when we disagree with them." That is, a Netflix that compromises with rogue-ish regimes is better for free expression than no Netflix at all.

One person outside the production, who was briefed on the deliberations in real time, told me Netflix discussed potential problems the episode would cause in Saudi Arabia before Mr. Minhaj filmed it, and raised the idea of scuttling it. This person would only speak on condition of anonymity because of the sensitive nature of the private discussions. An executive at the company, speaking on condition of anonymity for the same reason, said it only shared potential legal consequences with Mr. Minhaj's team as due diligence, noting it ultimately went forward with the show and its distribution in Saudi Arabia.

Until it didn't.

There have been other times when American businesses put American values above their bottom lines. After Steven Van Zandt, the E Street Band guitarist, led a musicians' boycott of South Africa to protest apartheid, corporations including Coca-Cola, General Electric and GTE followed suit by withdrawing from the country.

It's true that the entertainment industry did not bathe itself in glory during Hitler's early years.

But throughout the war and afterward, they, along with many other major American corporations, joined the robust national effort to defeat the Nazis and promote American values throughout Europe, which helped the United States win the Cold War.

It's a little hard to imagine such a national effort coming together now.

Maybe that's partly because the major social media and entertainment platforms have such global scale that they're almost their own borderless governments.

"It seems to be a moment in the evolution of the corporation that it starts to become akin to a world actor in its own right," Nicholas J. Cull, a professor at the University of Southern California's Annenberg School for Communication and Journalism who has written extensively on the American information effort during the Cold War. When it comes to their home country, he said, "It's, 'We're sympathetic, but we have our own set of interests.'"

The media behemoths would be wise to remember that their future growth will rely on having the same liberties that fostered their creation.

I'm reminded of a line from the Netflix-BBC One co-production of "Watership Down," based on Richard Adams's allegorical novel about a noble herd of rabbits' pursuit of a peaceful homeland. After their leader Hazel helps another group of rabbits escape a totalitarian warren, he tells them, "You have fought so hard to earn your freedom, but now you must fight to keep it, because the battle for liberty is one which has no end."

Take heed, Netflix.

JIM RUTENBERG writes the Mediator column for The New York Times.

A Warning to Saudis About What Happens to Dissidents

LETTER | THE NEW YORK TIMES | OCT. 23, 2018

A history professor says the Saudis are acting like Hitler, Mussolini, Stalin and other tyrants by killing a prominent opponent to send a message to the populace.

TO THE EDITOR:

In your excellent Oct. 19 editorial "Mr. Trump, Don't Back Down Now," you write that "contrary to Mr. Trump's suggestions, this was a crime against America." That is certainly the case, but the killing of Jamal Khashoggi was even more so a crime against the people of Saudi Arabia.

It was in its effect and probably in its intent an act of state terrorism that sent the following message to the kingdom's already intimidated people: We have just murdered a well-connected, powerful, prominent

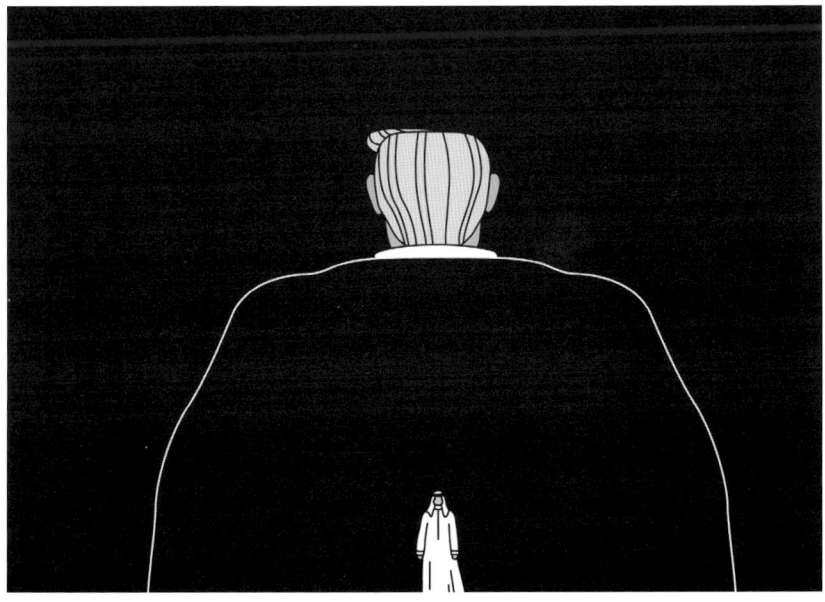

ROSE WONG

individual who dared to criticize us. It would be even easier for us to murder any one of you who may be foolish enough to voice criticism of our policies.

It is the same message previous tyrants have sent. Mussolini sent it when Fascists assassinated the opposition leader Giacomo Matteotti. Stalin sent it when he included prominent leaders of the Communist Party such as Nikolai Bukharin and Leon Trotsky in his purges. Hitler sent it when he had former Chancellor Kurt von Schleicher murdered. Mao Zedong sent it when people previously prominent in the Chinese Communist Party were sent to their deaths.

In each of these cases, and so many others, the tyrants knew that murders of the previously powerful sent a well-justified chill down the spines of millions.

Crown Prince Mohammed bin Salman appears to be following this barbaric policy of previous dictators.

JEFFREY HERF
College Park, Md.
The writer is a professor of history at the University of Maryland, College Park.

C.I.A. Concludes That Saudi Crown Prince Ordered Khashoggi Killed

BY JULIAN E. BARNES | NOV. 16, 2018

WASHINGTON — The Central Intelligence Agency has concluded that the Saudi crown prince, Mohammed bin Salman, ordered the killing of the journalist Jamal Khashoggi, according to American officials.

The C.I.A. made the assessment based on the crown prince's control of Saudi Arabia, which is such that the killing would not have taken place without his approval, and has buttressed its conclusion with two sets of crucial communications: intercepts of the crown prince's calls in the days before the killing, and calls by the kill team to a senior aide to the crown prince.

The C.I.A. has believed for weeks that Prince Mohammed was culpable in Mr. Khashoggi's killing but had been hesitant to definitively conclude that he directly ordered it. The agency has passed that assessment on to lawmakers and Trump administration officials.

The change in C.I.A. thinking came as new information emerged, officials said. The evidence included an intercept showing a member of the kill team calling an aide to Prince Mohammed and saying "tell your boss" that the mission was accomplished. Officials cautioned, however, that the new information is not direct evidence linking Prince Mohammed to the assassination, which was carried out in the Saudi Consulate in Istanbul.

The intercepts do show that Prince Mohammed was trying to find ways to lure Mr. Khashoggi back to Saudi Arabia, although the crown prince did not specifically say in the phone calls that he wanted to have Mr. Khashoggi killed, according to people briefed on the intelligence findings.

One former official said intelligence agencies were also examining communications between Mr. Khashoggi and the Saudi ambassador to Washington, Prince Khalid bin Salman, the brother of the crown prince.

MOHAMMED AL-SHAIKH/STRINGER/AFP/GETTY IMAGES

The journalist Jamal Khashoggi in December 2014 in Bahrain.

Prince Khalid's denial was unusually swift. In a Twitter post on Friday, he said that "the last contact" he had with Mr. Khashoggi was by text on Oct. 26, 2017, and that he never suggested that Mr. Khashoggi go to Turkey.

"I never talked to him by phone and certainly never suggested he go to Turkey for any reason," he tweeted.

The C.I.A.'s assessment was first reported Friday by The Washington Post. A C.I.A. spokesman declined to comment.

The increasingly definitive assessment from the spy agency creates a problem for President Trump, who has tied his administration to Prince Mohammed and proclaimed him the future of Saudi Arabia, a longtime American ally.

But the new assessment by the C.I.A. is sure to harden the resolve of lawmakers on Capitol Hill to continue to investigate the killing of Mr. Khashoggi and punish Saudi Arabia.

Jared Kushner, the president's son-in-law and senior adviser, has been particularly close to Prince Mohammed. Mr. Kushner has long advocated that a strong relationship with the Saudis is in the United States' interest, and he has pushed to maintain support for the crown prince despite the death of Mr. Khashoggi, who Saudi officials now say was killed with a lethal dose of tranquilizers and dismembered. Previously, Saudi officials said that Mr. Khashoggi had been strangled.

Neither administration officials nor intelligence officers believe the controversy over Mr. Khashoggi will drive Prince Mohammed from power, which is one reason White House officials believe cutting ties with the prince would not be in the interest of the United States.

"It is one of those acts that must cause us to re-examine the relationship and how much dependence we place on it," said Representative Adam B. Schiff, Democrat of California, who is set to lead the House Intelligence Committee next year.

Senate Republicans, according to people briefed on their deliberations, want to see more decisive steps from Saudi Arabia to try to defuse the crisis. One move that could blunt tougher congressional action, they said, would be for Riyadh to release some dissidents, including the leaders of the effort to allow Saudi women to drive.

Lawmakers are hoping to use the controversy over the assassination to try to force an end to the Saudi war in Yemen, or at least the American military support for it.

The United States has already announced that it would end air-refueling flights for the Saudi Air Force over Yemen, and it has sanctioned 17 Saudis for their alleged involvement in the killing of Mr. Khashoggi.

Mr. Schiff said the Trump administration's move to cut off refueling for Saudi planes conducting airstrikes is more significant than the sanctions.

"If we truly want to affect Saudi behavior, it is going to be more important to focus on bringing an end to the campaign in Yemen than these announcements of sanctions on these individuals we are unlikely to be able to reach," he said.

Mr. Schiff said he was pushing for a classified briefing for the entire House on the war in Yemen and American support for the Saudi campaign. Congressional Republicans have also said they would support such a briefing.

Skepticism in Congress about the Saudis has grown as Saudi officials have given multiple and conflicting accounts of what happened in the consulate in Istanbul. This week, they announced they would seek the death penalty against some of the perpetrators.

C.I.A. officials have long been unsure about Prince Mohammed and his abilities to lead the kingdom. The agency, and its former director, John O. Brennan, had a close relationship with Prince Mohammed's rival, Mohammed bin Nayef. The young crown prince outmaneuvered his rival in 2017 to consolidate his position.

Turkish officials made tape recordings of the killing of Mr. Khashoggi in the consulate, and the Turkish government was the first to say that it had definitive proof that Mr. Khashoggi was assassinated.

But Turkish officials have stopped short of saying there is definitive evidence of Prince Mohammed's role in the death on the recordings they have.

Saudi King Stands by Crown Prince as Outrage Over Khashoggi Killing Spreads

BY BEN HUBBARD AND CARLOTTA GALL | NOV. 19, 2018

BEIRUT, LEBANON — King Salman of Saudi Arabia on Monday stood by his son and crown prince, Mohammed bin Salman, avoiding any mention of the international outrage toward the kingdom in his first public remarks since Saudi agents killed the dissident journalist Jamal Khashoggi in Istanbul last month.

The echoes of that killing continued to spread Monday, with Germany imposing sanctions on 18 Saudis suspected of involvement and freezing arms exports to Saudi Arabia. And the Turkish defense minister suggested that Mr. Khashoggi's killers could have left the country with his body.

Mr. Khashoggi's killing inside the Saudi Consulate in Istanbul has become a lightning rod for Western criticism of Saudi Arabia, its human rights record and the leadership of Prince Mohammed, the kingdom's day-to-day ruler.

A growing chorus of current and former Western officials have concluded that an operation as elaborate as the one to kill Mr. Khashoggi could not have been carried out without the prince's knowledge. American officials told The New York Times and other publications last week that the C.I.A. had concluded that the prince had ordered the killing.

Saudi officials have vehemently denied that the crown prince had any involvement in the death of Mr. Khashoggi, a Virginia resident who wrote columns for The Washington Post that were critical of some Saudi policies. They have portrayed the killing as a result of a rogue operation to return Mr. Khashoggi to Saudi Arabia.

The heightened scrutiny of Prince Mohammed, 33, has caused speculation in some quarters that he could be pushed aside. But in Saudi

Crown Prince Mohammed bin Salman in Riyadh, Oct. 24, 2018.

Arabia's absolute monarchy, only his father has the authority to do so, and in Monday's remarks, he showed no intention to sideline his son.

In his annual address to the Shura Council, the kingdom's advisory assembly, the 82-year-old monarch stuck to general statements on official Saudi policy, calling on the world to stop Iran's nuclear program, press for political solutions to the wars in Syria and Yemen, and keep up the fight against terrorism.

If the king made any reference to the aftermath of Mr. Khashoggi's killing, it was done obliquely.

He praised the country's public prosecutor, whose office is handling the official Saudi investigation into the killing. Last week, the prosecutor's office said that it had filed criminal charges against 11 Saudis for suspected involvement in the killing and that it was seeking the death penalty against five of them, usually carried out in Saudi Arabia by beheading.

"We affirm that this country will never deviate from the application of Allah's law without any distinction or delay," the king said.

He also made a vague reference to governmental reforms to ensure that instructions are properly followed to "avoid any violations or mistakes."

Saudi Arabia has said that the operation that led to Mr. Khashoggi's death was carried out outside the chain of command. Last month, King Salman announced the formation of a committee charged with restructuring the intelligence apparatus to prevent similar problems from occurring in the future.

Heading that committee is Prince Mohammed.

Those steps have done little to cast doubt on the narrative laid out by Turkish officials that Mr. Khashoggi was suffocated soon after entering the consulate and then dismembered by a team of 15 Saudi agents who had flown in to do the job. Nor have the kingdom's frequently shifting explanations stemmed the outrage in Western countries over the death.

Germany on Monday froze the delivery of previously approved arms exports to Saudi Arabia over the killing of Mr. Khashoggi. It also barred 18 Saudis from entering Europe's border-free Schengen zone because of their suspected involvement.

Heiko Maas, the German foreign minister, told reporters in Brussels that his country had issued the ban for the 26-nation zone in close coordination with France, which is part of the Schengen area, and Britain, which is not.

"As before, there are more questions than answers in this case, with the crime itself and who is behind it," Mr. Maas said.

Over the weekend, the United States announced sanctions on 17 Saudis suspected of involvement in the killing. The German list included the same names, plus that of Gen. Ahmed Asiri, the former deputy head of Saudi intelligence, who was fired after Mr. Khashoggi was killed.

Mr. Khashoggi, 59, went to the consulate in Istanbul on Oct. 2 to obtain papers that would allow him to marry his fiancée, who is Turkish.

Over the past few weeks, the Turks have leaked evidence of the plot, including the names and photographs of the Saudi team members and surveillance footage of them arriving at the airport and moving around in Istanbul.

The Turkish defense minister provided further information over the weekend, pressing the case that the team had set out to kill Mr. Khashoggi, rather than deciding to do so only after an effort to bring him home had failed, as Saudi officials have contended.

"The most important issue is this crime was premeditated, it did not happen in a second," the minister, Hulusi Akar, said at the Halifax International Security Forum in Canada on Saturday. "It was premeditated. Those people were sent to Istanbul and they did their work."

Mr. Akar also provided a new possible answer to one of the killing's enduring mysteries — the location of Mr. Khashoggi's remains — suggesting that the Saudi agents could have carried Mr. Khashoggi's dismembered body out of the country in their luggage under the cover of diplomatic immunity.

"Possibly, possibly they committed the murder and then after that, within three or four hours, they left Turkey," said Mr. Akar, a retired general who left his post as chief of staff in the summer to take up the civilian post of defense minister.

"And because of the diplomatic immunity they left very easily, without having any problem with the luggage," he added. "Possibly in the luggage they carried the dismembered body of Khashoggi."

The killers had several hours between Mr. Khashoggi's arrival at the consulate and the time when his fiancée and friends alerted the Turkish authorities that he had not emerged, Mr. Akar noted. By then, Mr. Khashoggi's body had probably already been removed from the consulate, he said.

"Possibly, Khashoggi was strangled as soon as he entered and after that dismembered. And they removed the body parts from the consulate," he said. "Turkish teams did some work in the consulate but they could find nothing."

Turkish officials have said that most of the 15 Saudis who arrived in Istanbul by commercial and private planes in the hours before the killing did not have diplomatic status. When they left, their luggage passed through airport security machines. Security officers also hand-searched some of the luggage on the second plane.

At least nine of the Saudis were government and security officials. One, Maher Abdulaziz Mutreb, was a frequent companion of Prince Mohammed.

A diplomat who left shortly after the killing was an intelligence officer and the deputy head of the Saudi consulate, Ahmad Abdullah al-Muzaini. Mr. Muzaini made a quick trip to Riyadh, the Saudi capital, after Mr. Khashoggi first visited the consulate on Sept. 28. He returned to Istanbul the day before the killing and was photographed passing through Ataturk Airport, which serves the city, with heavy luggage.

He left the country again at 9:35 p.m. on the evening of the death, flying direct to Riyadh from Sabiha Gokcen Airport on Istanbul's Asian side, according to security camera footage released to the Turkish news media. The Saudi consul, Mohammad al-Otaibi, who was also at the consulate during the killing, left the country two weeks later.

BEN HUBBARD reported from Beirut, and **CARLOTTA GALL** from Istanbul.
KARAM SHOUMALI contributed reporting from Berlin.

The War on Truth Spreads

EDITORIAL | BY THE NEW YORK TIMES | DEC. 9, 2018

Democratically elected leaders borrow from the anti-press playbook of dictators and tyrants.

The editorial board represents the opinions of the board, its editor and the publisher. It is separate from the newsroom and the Op-Ed section.

A FREE AND UNFETTERED news media has long been anathema to authoritarian rulers, but even George Orwell might not have anticipated that some of the most unscrupulous assaults on press freedoms would one day be perpetrated by democratically elected governments. Witness these recent events:

Earlier this week Maria Ressa, founder of an online news site critical of the Philippine government of President Rodrigo Duterte, turned herself in to face charges of tax evasion on her return from receiving an International Press Freedom Award from the Committee to Protect Journalists. Mr. Duterte has long harassed Ms. Ressa and her start-up, Rappler, and other independent media critical of his murderous campaign against drug dealers and drug users. At one news conference, Mr. Duterte warned a Rappler reporter not to come to his hometown, Davao City, because "something bad will happen to you." Davao is thought to be home to the most vicious of Philippine vigilante bands, the Davao Death Squad.

The week before, more than 400 news outlets in Hungary, including the leading online newspaper and all remaining regional newspapers, were "donated" by their owners — many of them oligarchs loyal to Prime Minister Viktor Orban who had been systematically buying up outlets — to a foundation run by Mr. Orban's cronies. Poland under the nationalist Law and Justice Party has been stymied by civil society in its more brazen attempts to emulate Hungary, but the public broadcaster has become something of an ideological mouthpiece.

The infamous state-ordered murder of Jamal Khashoggi, a Washington Post columnist and critic of the Saudi crown prince, is in a class of its own, and Saudi Arabia is emphatically not a democracy, illiberal or otherwise. But President Trump, the leader of the world's premier democracy, has added to his other trespasses against the press by refusing to criticize the kingdom and Crown Prince Mohammed bin Salman, despite evidence that the powerful heir must have been behind the grisly execution.

President Trump's own assault on the press includes his trademark dismissal of any reporting that riles him as "fake news" and his inflammatory depiction of the news media as the "enemy of the people." His attempt to strip White House press credentials from CNN's Jim Acosta on the phony pretext that he had "laid hands" on a White House intern may not be in the same league as the exploits of other autocratic press bashers — the credentials were restored by a judge in a heartening affirmation of America's legal institutions and the First Amendment — but the president's disdain for fact, immunity to shame and inability to stomach criticism have offered solace to illiberal comrades.

Some of the most ardent hand-wringing over Mr. Khashoggi's murder was in Turkey, where he was killed. "The fate of Khashoggi is a test for the whole world with respect to freedom of expression," tweeted former Prime Minister Ahmet Davutoglu. Yet Turkey, under President Recep Tayyip Erdogan, holds the world record for throwing journalists in prison.

The rise of democratically elected leaders who seek to subjugate the media to their emergent cults of personality, combined with veteran masters of repression like China or Russia, has made life far more difficult for honest journalists and news outlets. But even for the old pros, times have changed.

Back in the days when news was printed on paper or broadcast over radio and television, authoritarian powers like the Soviet Union and its ideological replicants simply seized control of the outlets, censored what came in from outside and repressed anyone who spoke out. The methods were crudely effective, but they also endowed smuggled-in news with the credibility of the forbidden.

New information technologies — the internet, social media, smartphone cameras — were supposed to overcome censorship. They did, but they also armed autocrats with new ways to undermine the credibility of honest news. Fake news — the really fake kind — has proliferated, along with notions such as "alternative facts."

When they founded Rappler in 2012, Ms. Ressa and her colleagues thought they would use the internet to give the powerless a voice. Instead, the internet in the Philippines of Mr. Duterte has become an outlet for threats and deceit, and much of Rappler's efforts have been dedicated to uncovering the lies planted on the web by the president's allies and pointing them out to Facebook, the source of almost all internet news in the Philippines. It's a losing battle — false news is so rooted in the Philippines that one Facebook executive has called it "patient zero" in the global misinformation epidemic.

And yet Ms. Ressa fights on, as do reporters the world over, exposing abuse, lies and false reporting. That's the good news.

Glossary

anathema Something that is strongly disliked.

anti-vaccine activists Individuals and like-minded groups who oppose medical vaccination.

authoritarianism A form of government characterized by strong central power and limited political freedoms. Individual freedoms are subordinate to the state and there is no constitutional accountability under an authoritarian regime.

authoritarian regime Any government that concentrates political power in an authority not responsible to the people.

The Bureau of Censorship Also known as the Office of Censorship, this was a wartime censoring arm of the executive branch during the World War II. The office was principally staffed by former members of the press.

censorship The suppression or prohibition of any parts of books, films, news, etc. that are considered obscene, politically unacceptable or a threat to security.

consulate Similar to an embassy, this is an area where matters pertaining to one country can be addressed within the territory of another. A consulate typically deals with individuals or businesses.

digital activism Also known as cyberactivism, this form of activism relies upon the Internet and digital media as key platforms for mass mobilization and political action.

dissident A person who opposes official policy, especially that of an authoritarian state, or who is opposed to an official policy.

Espionage Act Also known as the Espionage Bill, this law was enacted by Congress on June 15, 1917. It was one of several contemporary acts that granted sweeping wartime censorship powers to the U.S. government in the name of national defense.

exposé A piece of writing that reveals the true nature or circumstances of something.

gag order A directive from a court or government restricting the dissemination of information to the public.

libel A published piece of writing that is false and damaging to the reputation of a person or group.

oppression The prolonged cruel or unjust treatment or control of an individual or group.

propaganda The spread of information or ideas to further a political agenda. To that end, misinformation, exaggerations and selective facts are often used to sway public opinion.

suppression The act of forcibly preventing, inhibiting or otherwise eliminating something, such as an activity or publication.

transparency The condition of operating in a clear way so that others can see and understand the actions being performed.

unscrupulous Lacking morals or principles.

Media Literacy Terms

"Media literacy" refers to the ability to access, understand, critically assess and create media. The following terms are important components of media literacy, and they will help you critically engage with the articles in this title.

angle The aspect of a news story that a journalist focuses on and develops.

attribution The method by which a source is identified or by which facts and information are assigned to the person who provided them.

balance Principle of journalism that both perspectives of an argument should be presented in a fair way.

bias A disposition of prejudice in favor of a certain idea, person or perspective.

column A type of story that is a regular feature, often on a recurring topic, written by the same journalist, generally known as a columnist.

commentary A type of story that is an expression of opinion on recent events by a journalist generally known as a commentator.

credibility The quality of being trustworthy and believable, said of a journalistic source.

critical review A type of story that describes an event or work of art, such as a theater performance, film, concert, book, restaurant, radio or television program, exhibition or musical piece, and offers critical assessment of its quality and reception.

editorial Article of opinion or interpretation.

feature story Article designed to entertain as well as to inform.

human interest story A type of story that focuses on individuals and how events or issues affect their life, generally offering a sense of relatability to the reader.

impartiality Principle of journalism that a story should not reflect a journalist's bias and should contain balance.

intention The motive or reason behind something, such as the publication of a news story.

motive The reason behind something, such as the publication of a news story or a source's perspective on an issue.

news story An article or style of expository writing that reports news, generally in a straightforward fashion and without editorial comment.

op-ed An opinion piece that reflects a prominent individual's opinion on a topic of interest.

paraphrase The summary of an individual's words, with attribution, rather than a direct quotation of their exact words.

plagiarism An attempt to pass another person's work as one's own without attribution.

reliability The quality of being dependable and accurate, said of a journalistic source.

rhetorical device Technique in writing intending to persuade the reader or communicate a message from a certain perspective.

source The origin of the information reported in journalism.

style A distinctive use of language in writing or speech; also a news or publishing organization's rules for consistent use of language with regard to spelling, punctuation, typography and capitalization, usually regimented by a house style guide.

tone A manner of expression in writing or speech.

Media Literacy Questions

1. Identify each of the sources in "Conflicting Censorship Upsets Many Journalists" (on page 34) as a primary source or a secondary source. Evaluate the reliability and credibility of each source. How does your evaluation of each source change your perspective on this article?

2. Kareem Fahim's article "Egypt Officials Stop Facebook Program for Free Access to Internet" (on page 45) and Yasmine El Rashidi's article "How Egypt Crowdsources Censorship" (on page 47) are both about censorship efforts in Egypt. Are there differences in the style and tone of each article?

3. Identify the various sources cited in the article "Turks Click Away, but Wikipedia Is Gone" (on page 52). How does Patrick Kingsley attribute information to each of these sources in his article? How effective are Kingsley's attributions in helping the reader identify his sources?

4. Identify each of the sources in "Reuters Publishes Account of Myanmar Massacre After Journalists' Arrests" (on page 61) as a primary source or a secondary source. Evaluate the reliability and credibility of each source. How does your evaluation of each source change your perspective on this article?

5. What type of story is "Seeing Terror Risk, U.S. Asks Journals to Cut Flu Study Facts" (on page 99)? Can you identify another article in this collection that is the same type of story? What elements helped you come to your conclusion?

6. Examine the headline of David French's op-ed "Conservatives Fail the N.F.L.'s Free Speech Test" (on page 117). How does this headline imply the angle French explores in the article's contents?

7. Does "Google Employees Protest Secret Work on Censored Search Engine for China" (on page 141) use multiple sources? What are the strengths of using multiple sources in a journalistic piece? What are the weaknesses of relying heavily on only one or a few sources?

8. The article "The Dangers of Digital Activism" (on page 145) is an example of an op-ed. Identify how Manal Al-Sharif's attitude and tone help convey her opinion on the topic.

9. "There May Soon Be Three Internets. America's Won't Necessarily Be the Best." (on page 148), "The Poison on Facebook and Twitter Is Still Spreading" (on page 153) and "The War on Truth Spreads" (on page 208) are all written by The New York Times Editorial Board. Each piece features an introduction clarifying the Board's views are separate from the newsroom and the op-ed section. What is the purpose of this clarification, particularly in the context of each article's subject matter?

10. Does Neil MacFarquhar demonstrate the journalistic principle of impartiality in his article " 'They Want to Block Our Future': Thousands Protest Russia's Internet Censorship" (on page 162)? If so, how does he do so? If not, what could MacFarquhar have included to make his article more impartial?

11. What is the angle of Paul Mozur's article "Twitter Users in China Face Detention and Threats in New Beijing Crackdown" (on page 187)? Compare it with the angle of Jim Rutenberg's article "Netflix's Bow to Saudi Censors Comes at a Cost to Free Speech" (on page 192).

12. "C.I.A. Concludes That Saudi Crown Prince Ordered Khashoggi Killed" (on page 199) features a photograph of Jamal Khashoggi. What does this photograph add to the article?

Citations

All citations in this list are formatted according to the Modern Language Association's (MLA) style guide.

BOOK CITATION

THE NEW YORK TIMES EDITORIAL STAFF. *Censorship: The Motives for Suppression.* New York: New York Times Educational Publishing, 2020.

ONLINE ARTICLE CITATIONS

ALBERTUS, MICHAEL, AND VICTOR MENALDO. "Why Are So Many Democracies Breaking Down?" *The New York Times*, 8 May 2018, https://www.nytimes.com/2018/05/08/opinion/democracy-authoritarian-constitutions.html.

AL-SHARIF, MANAL. "The Dangers of Digital Activism." *The New York Times*, 16 Sept. 2018, https://www.nytimes.com/2018/09/16/opinion/politics/the-dangers-of-digital-activism.html.

BARNES, JULIAN E. "C.I.A. Concludes That Saudi Crown Prince Ordered Khashoggi Killed." *The New York Times*, 16 Nov. 2018, https://www.nytimes.com/2018/11/16/us/politics/cia-saudi-crown-prince-khashoggi.html.

BROAD, WILLIAM J. "Science and Censorship: A Duel Lasting Centuries." *The New York Times*, 26 Dec. 2011, https://www.nytimes.com/2011/12/27/science/science-and-censorship-a-duel-lasting-centuries.html.

BROWNE, MALCOLM W. "Conflicting Censorship Upsets Many Journalists." *The New York Times*, 21 Jan. 1991, https://timesmachine.nytimes.com/timesmachine/1991/01/21/035491.html.

BUCKLEY, CHRIS. "After Criticism, Publisher Reverses Decision to Bow to China's Censors." *The New York Times*, 21 Aug. 2017, https://www.nytimes.com/2017/08/21/world/asia/china-quarterly-cambridge-university-press-censorship-publisher-reverses-decision-to-bow-to-chinas-censors.html.

CAVE, DAMIEN. "Australian Gag Order Stokes Global Debate on Secrecy." *The*

New York Times, 14 Dec. 2018, https://www.nytimes.com/2018/12/14/world/australia/australia-gag-order-court.html.

CONGER, KATE, AND DAISUKE WAKABAYASHI. "Google Employees Protest Secret Work on Censored Search Engine for China." *The New York Times*, 16 Aug. 2018, https://www.nytimes.com/2018/08/16/technology/google-employees-protest-search-censored-china.html.

CONNELLY, MARJORIE. "Who Likes Web Censorship? (Ask Putin.)" *The New York Times*, 22 Apr. 2014, https://www.nytimes.com/2014/04/23/upshot/who-likes-web-censorship-ask-putin.html.

DONADIO, RACHEL. "Is There Censorship?" *The New York Times*, 19 Dec. 2004, https://www.nytimes.com/2004/12/19/books/arts/essay-is-there-censorship.html.

EL RASHIDI, YASMINE. "How Egypt Crowdsources Censorship." *The New York Times*, 8 Dec. 2018, https://www.nytimes.com/2018/12/08/opinion/sunday/egypt-censorship-crowdsourcing.html.

FAHIM, KAREEM. "Egypt Officials Stop Facebook Program for Free Access to Internet." *The New York Times*, 30 Dec. 2015, https://www.nytimes.com/2015/12/31/world/middleeast/egypt-officials-stop-facebook-program-for-free-access-to-internet.html.

FISH, STANLEY. "Crying Censorship." *The New York Times*, 24 Aug. 2008, https://opinionator.blogs.nytimes.com/2008/08/24/crying-censorship/.

FRENCH, DAVID. "Conservatives Fail the N.F.L.'s Free Speech Test." *The New York Times*, 24 May 2018, https://www.nytimes.com/2018/05/24/opinion/conservatives-fail-the-nfls-free-speech-test.html.

GALL, CARLOTTA. "Erdogan's Next Target as He Restricts Turkey's Democracy: The Internet." *The New York Times*, 4 Mar. 2018, https://www.nytimes.com/2018/03/04/world/europe/turkey-erdogan-internet-law-restrictions.html.

GRADY, DENISE, AND WILLIAM J. BROAD. "Seeing Terror Risk, U.S. Asks Journals to Cut Flu Study Facts." *The New York Times*, 20 Dec. 2011, https://www.nytimes.com/2011/12/21/health/fearing-terrorism-us-asks-journals-to-censor-articles-on-virus.html.

GURIEV, SERGEI, AND DANIEL TREISMAN. "The New Dictators Rule by Velvet Fist." *The New York Times*, 24 May 2015, https://www.nytimes.com/2015/05/25/opinion/the-new-dictators-rule-by-velvet-fist.html.

HILGERS, LAUREN. "China's Oppression Reaches Beyond Its Borders." *The New York Times*, 9 Apr. 2018, https://www.nytimes.com/2018/04/09/opinion/china-oppression.html.

HUBBARD, BEN, AND CARLOTTA GALL. "Saudi King Stands by Crown Prince as Outrage Over Khashoggi Killing Spreads." *The New York Times*, 19 Nov. 2018, https://www.nytimes.com/2018/11/19/world/middleeast/saudi-arabia-king-salman-khashoggi.html.

KINGSLEY, PATRICK. "Turks Click Away, but Wikipedia Is Gone." *The New York Times*, 10 June 2017, https://www.nytimes.com/2017/06/10/world/europe/turkey-wikipedia-ban-recep-tayyip-erdogan.html.

KINGSLEY, PATRICK, AND BENJAMIN NOVAK. "The Website That Shows How a Free Press Can Die." *The New York Times*, 24 Nov. 2018, https://www.nytimes.com/2018/11/24/world/europe/hungary-viktor-orban-media.html.

LANSBERG-RODRÍGUEZ, DANIEL. "Stealth Censorship in Venezuela." *The New York Times*, 6 Aug. 2014, https://www.nytimes.com/2014/08/07/opinion/daniel-lansberg-rodriguez-stealth-censorship-in-venezuela.html.

MACFARQUHAR, NEIL. " 'They Want to Block Our Future': Thousands Protest Russia's Internet Censorship." *The New York Times*, 30 Apr. 2018, https://www.nytimes.com/2018/04/30/world/europe/russia-telegram-digital-resistance.html.

MANGUEL, ALBERTO. " 'Censors at Work,' by Robert Darnton." *The New York Times*, 7 Nov. 2014, https://www.nytimes.com/2014/11/09/books/review/censors-at-work-by-robert-darnton.html.

MANJOO, FARHAD. "Clearing Out the App Stores: Government Censorship Made Easier." *The New York Times*, 18 Jan. 2017, https://www.nytimes.com/2017/01/18/technology/clearing-out-the-app-stores-government-censorship-made-easier.html.

MARKEL, HOWARD. "Don't Censor Influenza Research." *The New York Times*, 1 Feb. 2012, https://www.nytimes.com/2012/02/02/opinion/censorship-hinders-influenza-research.html.

MOYER, MELINDA WENNER. "Anti-Vaccine Activists Have Taken Vaccine Science Hostage." *The New York Times*, 4 Aug. 2018, https://www.nytimes.com/2018/08/04/opinion/sunday/anti-vaccine-activists-have-taken-vaccine-science-hostage.html.

MOZUR, PAUL. "Twitter Users in China Face Detention and Threats in New Beijing Crackdown." *The New York Times*, 10 Jan. 2019, https://www.nytimes.com/2019/01/10/business/china-twitter-censorship-online.html.

NECHEPURENKO, IVAN. "In Russia, a Top University Lacks Just One Thing: Students." *The New York Times*, 26 Aug. 2018, https://www.nytimes.com/2018/08/26/world/europe/european-university-st-petersburg-russia.html.

THE NEW YORK TIMES. "Bullying and Censorship." *The New York Times*, 6 Dec. 2010, https://www.nytimes.com/2010/12/07/opinion/07tue4.html.

THE NEW YORK TIMES. "Censorship and Publicity." *The New York Times*, 16 Apr. 1917, https://timesmachine.nytimes.com/timesmachine/1917/04/16/102334163.html.

THE NEW YORK TIMES. "Censorship Bill Fought in House." *The New York Times*, 1 May 1917, https://timesmachine.nytimes.com/timesmachine/1917/05/01/102338989.html.

THE NEW YORK TIMES. "Censorship Bureau Comes to an End." *The New York Times*, 16 Nov. 1945, https://timesmachine.nytimes.com/timesmachine/1945/11/16/103603539.html.

THE NEW YORK TIMES. "An Effective Censorship." *The New York Times*, 10 Mar. 1917, https://timesmachine.nytimes.com/timesmachine/1917/03/10/98244954.html.

THE NEW YORK TIMES. "Plans for America: A War Censorship." *The New York Times*, 3 Jan. 1916, https://timesmachine.nytimes.com/timesmachine/1916/01/03/301831092.html.

THE NEW YORK TIMES. "The Poison on Facebook and Twitter Is Still Spreading." *The New York Times*, 19 Oct. 2018, https://www.nytimes.com/2018/10/19/opinion/facebook-twitter-journalism-misinformation.html.

THE NEW YORK TIMES. "There May Soon Be Three Internets. America's Won't Necessarily Be the Best." *The New York Times*, 15 Oct. 2018, https://www.nytimes.com/2018/10/15/opinion/internet-google-china-balkanization.html.

THE NEW YORK TIMES. "War Censorship." *The New York Times*, 24 Nov. 1942, https://timesmachine.nytimes.com/timesmachine/1942/11/24/85068767.html.

THE NEW YORK TIMES. "War Censorship Discussed by U.S." *The New York Times*, 16 Aug. 1965, https://www.nytimes.com/1965/08/16/archives/war-censorship-discussed-by-us-wheeler-cites-news-report-on-troops.html.

THE NEW YORK TIMES. "The War-Censorship Nuisance." *The New York Times*, 10 Apr. 1862, https://timesmachine.nytimes.com/timesmachine/1862/04/10/78684549.html.

THE NEW YORK TIMES. "The War on Truth Spreads." *The New York Times*, 9 Dec. 2018, https://www.nytimes.com/2018/12/09/opinion/media-duterte-maria-ressa.html.

THE NEW YORK TIMES. "A Warning to Saudis About What Happens to Dissidents." *The New York Times*, 23 Oct. 2018, https://www.nytimes.com/2018/10/23/opinion/letters/saudi-dissidents.html.

OLECK, JOAN. "A World Map to Outwit Web Censors." *The New York Times*, 26 June 2003, https://www.nytimes.com/2003/06/26/technology/a-world-map-to-outwit-web-censors.html.

PADDOCK, RICHARD C. "Reuters Publishes Account of Myanmar Massacre After Journalists' Arrests." *The New York Times*, 10 Feb. 2018, https://www.nytimes.com/2018/02/10/world/asia/reuters-myanmar-massacre-rohingya.html.

PIGMAN, LINCOLN. "Russia, Accused of Faking News, Unfurls Its Own 'Fake News' Bill." *The New York Times*, 22 July 2018, https://www.nytimes.com/2018/07/22/world/europe/russia-fake-news-law.html.

POWELL, JESSICA. "The Problem With Banning Pornography on Tumblr." *The New York Times*, 6 Dec. 2018, https://www.nytimes.com/2018/12/06/opinion/tumblr-adult-content-pornography-ban.html.

PRICE, BYRON. "The Censor Defends the Censorship." *The New York Times*, 11 Feb. 1945, https://timesmachine.nytimes.com/timesmachine/1945/02/11/305663962.html.

PROULX, NATALIE. "How Important Is Freedom of the Press?" *The New York Times*, 4 May 2018, https://www.nytimes.com/2018/05/04/learning/how-important-is-freedom-of-the-press.html.

RUTENBERG, JIM. "In Trump Era, Censorship May Start in the Newsroom." *The New York Times*, 17 Feb. 2017, https://www.nytimes.com/2017/02/17/business/media/trump-era-media-censorship.html.

RUTENBERG, JIM. "Netflix's Bow to Saudi Censors Comes at a Cost to Free Speech." *The New York Times*, 6 Jan. 2019, https://www.nytimes.com/2019/01/06/business/media/netflix-saudi-arabia-censorship-hasan-minhaj.html.

THOMPSON, ERIN. "Art Censorship at Guantánamo Bay." *The New York Times*, 27 Nov. 2017, https://www.nytimes.com/2017/11/27/opinion/guantanamo-art-prisoners.html.

WEIWEI, AI. "Ai Weiwei: How Censorship Works." *The New York Times*, 6 May 2017, https://www.nytimes.com/2017/05/06/opinion/sunday/ai-weiwei-how-censorship-works.html.

WILLIAMS, JACQUELINE. "Australian Furor Over Chinese Influence Follows Book's Delay." *The New York Times*, 20 Nov. 2017, https://www.nytimes.com/2017/11/20/world/australia/china-australia-book-influence.html.

Index

A

Aftergood, Steven, 104–105, 107–108
Akdeniz, Yaman, 52–53
Albertus, Michael, 64–68
Altiparmak, Karem, 56, 58, 59
anti-vaxxers, 112–116
Apple, 128, 129–130, 131, 193
apps, 128–132
Arslan, Ahmet, 58
art censorship, 76–82, 83–86, 87, 88–92, 93–96, 97–98, 175–179
Australia, 93–96, 120–124
authoritarian regimes, 9, 37–40, 41–44, 45–46, 47–51, 52–54, 55–60, 61–63, 64–68, 69–75, 160–161

B

Barnes, Julian E., 199–202
Belongia, Edward, 115
Blume, Judy, 76–77
Broad, William J., 99–103, 104–108
Browne, Malcolm W., 34–36
Buckley, Chris, 180–182
bullying, 87
Bureau of Censorship, 31
Bush, George W./Bush administration, 81, 84, 107, 108, 110

C

Cambridge University Press, 96, 180–182
Casey, Rick, 134, 136, 137
Cave, Damien, 120–124
censorship
 and anti-vaxxers, 112–116
 and apps, 128–132
 and the arts, 76–82, 83–86, 87, 88–92, 93–96, 97–98, 175–179
 and authoritarian regimes, 9, 37–40, 41–44, 45–46, 47–51, 52–54, 55–60, 61–63, 64–68, 69–75, 160–161
 and bullying, 87
 and Civil War, 11–12
 defined, 8
 and flu virus, 99–103, 104–108, 109–111
 and L.G.B.T.Q. community, 157–159
 literary, 76–82, 83–86, 88–92, 93–96
 military, 32–33, 34–36
 online, 52–54, 55–60, 69–75, 125–127, 128–132, 141–144, 160–161, 162–165
 and Persian Gulf War, 34–36
 and pornography, 157–159
 and science, 99–103, 104–108, 109–111, 112–116
 self-censorship, 8–9, 84, 96, 99, 112, 176–177
 and social media, 45–46, 88, 128, 142, 145–147, 153–156, 157–159, 166–168, 184, 186, 187–191, 193
 and Vietnam War, 32–33, 34–36
 voluntary, 20, 22, 31, 32, 83–84, 106, 177
 in wartime, 8–9, 11–12, 13–15, 16–17, 18, 19–21, 22–23, 24–30, 31, 32–33, 34–36
 and World War I, 13–15, 16–17, 18, 19–21
 and World War II, 22–23, 24–30, 31, 118
Central Intelligence Agency (C.I.A.), 199–202, 203
Chávez, Hugo, 38, 39, 40, 41
China, 91–92, 93–96, 128–132, 141–144, 148–149, 150, 151, 175–179, 180–182, 183–186, 187–191
China Quarterly, The, 96, 180–182
Civil War, 11–12
Committee on Public Information, 18
Conger, Kate, 141–144
Connelly, Marjorie, 160–161
Creel, George, 18

D

Darnton, Robert, 88-92
Dede, Baris, 52, 54
Deibert, Ronald J., 127
digital activism, 145-147
Dragonfly, 141-144, 150, 151

E

Ebadi, Shirin, 78, 79, 80, 81
Egypt, 45-46, 47-51
El Rashidi, Yasmine, 47-51
Emerson, Arthur Rojas, 134, 136-137
Erdogan, Recep Tayyip, 42, 53, 55-60, 66, 67, 88, 139, 209
Espionage Act, 18, 19-21
European Union, 148-149
European University (St. Petersburg, Russia), 169-174

F

Facebook, 45-46, 153-156, 157-158, 188, 193
Fahim, Kareem, 45-46
fake news, 166-168, 209, 210
First Amendment, 8, 18, 84, 85, 122
Fish, Stanley, 83-86
flu virus, 99-103, 104-108, 109-111
France, 88-90, 167
Free Basics, 45-46
Freedom House, 39, 70
freedom of speech, 8, 84, 117-119
freedom of the press, 8, 138-140
in wartime, 8-9, 11-12, 13-15, 16-17, 18, 19-21, 22-23, 24-30, 31, 32-33, 34-36

G

Galileo, 106
Gall, Carlotta, 55-60, 203-207
Galperin, Eva, 131-132
German Democratic Republic, 88, 91
Giacomo, Carol, 139, 140
Google, 88, 128, 129-130, 131, 141-144, 150, 151, 188
Grady, Denise, 99-103
Guantánamo Bay, 97-98
Guriev, Sergei, 41-44

H

Hamilton, Clive, 93-96
Hein, Christoph, 91
Hilgers, Lauren, 183-186
Hubbard, Ben, 203-207
Hungary, 67, 69-75, 208

I

India, 46, 88, 90-91
Internet, 125-127, 128-132, 141-144, 148-152, 160-161, 162-165

J

journalists, 35, 57, 61-63

K

Kaepernick, Colin, 117
Kart, Musa, 138-139
Kenya, 167
Khashoggi, Jamal, 9, 192, 194, 197, 199-202, 203-207, 209
Kingsley, Patrick, 52-54, 69-75
Kushner, Jared, 200-201

L

Lansberg-Rodríguez, Daniel, 37-40
L.G.B.T.Q. community, 157-159
LinkedIn, 128, 188-189
literary censorship, 76-82, 83-86, 88-92, 93-96

M

MacFarquhar, Neil, 162-165
Maduro, Nicolás, 38, 40
Malaysia, 41, 167
Manguel, Alberto, 88-92
Manjoo, Farhad, 128-132
Markel, Howard, 109-111
Menaldo, Victor, 64-68
military censorship, 32-33, 34-36
Moglen, Eben, 128-129, 132
Mong, Attila, 70, 71
Moyer, Melinda Wenner, 112-116
Mozur, Paul, 187-191
Myanmar, 61-63, 65-66, 148, 153, 154-155

N

Nafisi, Azar, 81, 82
National Football League (N.F.L.), 117-119
Navalny, Aleksei A., 43, 163
Nechepurenko, Ivan, 169-174
Netflix, 192-196
New York Times, The, 11-12, 13-15, 16-17, 18, 19-21, 22-23, 31, 32-33, 36, 87, 122, 128-132, 138, 148-152, 153-156, 193, 197-198, 208-210
Novak, Benjamin, 69-75

O

Offit, Paul, 115
Oktar, Adnan, 55
Oleck, Joan, 125–127

INDEX **223**

online content, 52–54, 55–60, 69–75, 125–127, 128–132, 141–144, 160–161, 162–165
Orban, Viktor, 42, 67, 69–70, 71–72, 73, 75
Origo, 69–75
Osterholm, Michael, 116

P

Paddock, Richard C., 61–63
Patriot Act, 77, 78, 82
Paylan, Garo, 59, 60
Persian Gulf War, 34–36
Philippines, 208, 210
Pigman, Lincoln, 166–168
Poland, Gregory, 115
pornography, 157–159
Powell, Jessica, 157–159
Price, Byron, 24–30, 31
Proulx, Natalie, 138–140
Putin, Vladimir/Putin administration, 43, 160–161, 162, 164, 166, 169

R

Read, Andrew, 114
Reuters, 45, 61–63, 138–139
Rushdie, Salman, 79–80, 83
Russia, 128, 160–161, 162–165, 166–168, 169–174, 184
Rutenberg, Jim, 133–134, 136–137, 192–196

S

Salman, Mohammed bin, 192, 194, 198, 199–202, 203–207, 209
Saudi Arabia, 145–147, 192–196, 197–198, 199–202, 203–207
science, 99–103, 104–108, 109–111, 112–116
Scott, Hugh L., 13–15
Seaver, Richard, 79, 80
self-censorship, 8–9, 84, 96, 99, 112, 176–177
Sharif, Manal al-, 145–147
Siems, Larry, 77, 81
Simonsen, Lone, 113
Sisi, Abdel Fattah el-, 45, 50
Skowronski, Danuta, 114
Smith, Evan, 136
Smith, Lamar, 133–134
Smithsonian National Portrait Gallery, 87
social media, 45–46, 88, 128, 142, 145–147, 153–156, 157–159, 166–168, 184, 186, 187–191, 193

T

Telegram, 162–165
Thompson, Erin, 97–98
Treisman, Daniel, 41–44
Trump, Donald/Trump administration, 64, 69, 133–134, 136–137, 140, 151, 167, 194, 197, 200, 201, 209

Tumblr, 157–159
Turkey, 52–54, 55–60, 66–67, 139, 209
Twitter, 88, 142, 146–147, 153–156, 157–158, 184, 186, 187–191

V

Venezuela, 37–40, 41
Vietnam War, 32–33, 34–36
voluntary censorship, 20, 22, 31, 32, 83–84, 106, 177

W

Wakabayashi, Daisuke, 141–144
war on truth, 208–210
wartime censorship, 8–9, 11–12, 13–15, 16–17, 18, 19–21, 22–23, 24–30, 31, 32–33, 34–36
Weiwei, Ai, 175–179
Wheeler, Earle G., 32–33
Wikipedia, 52–54, 59
Williams, Jacqueline, 93–96
Wojnarowicz, David, 87
World War I, 13–15, 16–17, 18, 19–21
World War II, 22–23, 24–30, 31, 118

Z

Zhuang, Liehong, 183–185, 186
Zittrain, Jonathan, 126–127
Zuckerberg, Mark, 46

This book is current up until the time of printing. For the most up-to-date reporting, visit www.nytimes.com.